WINNING

The Mental Way

Karlene Sugarman, M.A.

A practical guide to team building and mental training

Step Up Publishing
Burlingame, CA 94010

WINNING THE MENTAL WAY

Printed and bound in the United States of America.

Published by: Step Up Publishing
1312 Drake Avenue
Burlingame, CA 94010

ISBN: 0-9666661-9-4
Library of Congress Catalog Number: 98-90653

pp. 24, 27, Reprinted with permission of Simon & Schuster from AWAKEN THE GIANT WITHIN by Anthony Robbins. Copyright © 1991 by Anthony Robbins.

pp. 37, 45, From NAPOLEON HILL'S KEYS TO SUCCESS by Napoleon Hill. Copyright © 1994 by The Napoleon Hill Foundation. Used by permission of Dutton Signet, a division of Penguin Putnam Inc.

pp. 39, 171, 175, Reprinted with permission of Simon & Schuster from UNLIMITED POWER by Anthony Robbins. Copyright © 1986 by Robbins Research Institute.

pp. 43, 57, 71, 76, Reprinted with permission of Oxford University Press from SUN TZU THE ART OF WAR by Sun Tzu. Copyright © 1963.

p. 82, Reprinted with the permission of Simon & Schuster from FOOTBALL'S GREATEST QUOTES by Bob Chieger and Pat Sullivan. Copyright © 1990 by Bob Chieger and Pat Sullivan.

p. 12, Reprinted with the permission of Simon & Schuster from OUTRAGEOUS by Charles Barkley and R.S. Johnson. Copyright © 1992 by Charles Barkley and R.S. Johnson.

p. 72, Reprinted with the permission of Simon & Schuster from HOW TO WIN FRIENDS AND INFLUENCE PEOPLE by Dale Carnegie. Copyright © 1936 by Dale Carnegie. Copyright renewed 1964 by Donna Dale Carnegie and reprinted by Simon & Schuster. Revised edition renewed 1964 by Donna Dale Carnegie and Dorothy Carnegie.

pp. 97, 189, Reprinted by permission of Jeremy P. Tarcher, Inc, a division of The Putnam Publishing Group from SPORTS PSYCHING by Thomas Tutko, Ph.D. and Umberto Tosi. Copyright © 1976 by Thomas Tutko and Umberto Tosi.

p. 76, Reprinted with permission of St. Martin's Press, Incorporated from THE ART OF WINNING by Dennis Conner. Copyright © 1988 by Dennis Conner.

p. 60, Reprinted with permission of St. Martin's Press, Incorporated from BUILDING A CHAMPION by Bill Walsh with Glenn Dickey. Copyright © 1990 by Bill Walsh.

pp. 11, 15, 18, 107, 115 146, Reprinted with permission from THE MENTAL GAME OF BASEBALL: A guide to peak performance by H.A. Dorfman and Karl Kuehl. Copyright © 1989, 1995.

pp. 22, 23, 120, Reprinted with permission from TAO TE CHING translated by Stephen Mitchell by HarperCollins Publishers. Translation copyright © 1988.

p. 165, Concentration Grid adapted by permission from American Coaching Effectiveness Program, 1989, Sport Psychology Workbook (Champaign, IL: Human Kinetics), 131.

Photographs courtesy of University of San Francisco Athletics
pp. 41, 44, 65, 81, 97 by Takamoro Nagahama
p. 71 by Gerry Cantu

ACKNOWLEDGMENTS

To my friends and family, thank you for your constant support and encouragement.

To everyone who took part in this project, thank you for sharing your invaluable knowledge and insight.

TABLE OF CONTENTS

WORDS FROM AUTHOR

Having been a competitive athlete (figure skater) for 10 years. I know the importance of the mental side of sports – it's too bad I didn't pay more attention to it then! I know the frustration of being near perfect one day and terrible the next. Although, at that time, there wasn't too much emphasis placed on mental practice. Fortunately that seems to be changing. But the resources out there seem to do just that – focus on the individual athlete, not on the psychology of the team, or if they do, they tend to be sport specific. In that lies the seed that was planted for the premise of this book.

I think the thing that motivated me to write this book was the fact that there aren't many books out there on sports psychology with a team emphasis; educating the readers on how a team can best function and how to be successful on a more consistent basis. Having a team that is mentally prepared is more than getting a group of individuals together, it is getting the team to operate as **one** unit. Walking around the book stores you see very few sports psychology books; the ones that you normally do see are self-help books, how work groups function, motivational books, and performance enhancement for the **individual** athlete. Also, the books on teams tend to be for business groups or on the social aspect of sports, as opposed to the mental aspect. None of them really combine all of these factors. That is the mission behind this book – to provide tools for teams and individuals wishing to reach their full potential.

I approached this book the same way I ask athletes to approach their sport. Have a dream, something that you want to make a reality; uncover your mission or creed that will keep you going; and set long-term, short-term and daily goals to get you there. Then, implement performance enhancement techniques to help with the journey i.e., relaxation, imagery, concentration and positive self-talk. And, find ways to deal with obstacles that may stand in the way of reaching your goals i.e., slumps, choking, distractions, injuries, etc. I feel the process of writing this book has improved my abilities as a Sports Psychology Consultant tremendously. It has been a while since I was competing, but this book venture conjured up all the same feelings (and distractions) that come with wanting to achieve peak performance in an endeavor.

I think the stigma surrounding sports psychology as only necessary for those athletes with "problems" is fading. Sports psychology is for anyone who wants to improve their performance in any endeavor they take on. People are finally seeing the benefits it can provide for all athletes and teams. And, giving athletes knowledge that they can apply day-in and day-out, on and off the field is what brings me the most satisfaction. It is **my** passion. I am lucky to have found my passion and am pursuing this path. I want others to be able to do the same and feel the **same** satisfaction. The same fulfillment that I felt the day this book was completed. By reading this book with a strong commitment to improving your ability to be a mentally tough team player you will be taking a big step towards improving your performance – as a coach, player, executive. It's a long journey, there will be no instant results, only slow subtle changes. Remember – patience is a virtue! ***Good Luck!!!***

Introduction
Why Team Building and Mental Training?

The way a team performs is contingent on many group dynamics. Group dynamics is an area dedicated to advancing knowledge and the nature of groups, the laws of development, and their interrelations with individuals (Cartwright & Zander, 1968). Research in group dynamics has focused on such topics as group performance, interpersonal relations in teams, leadership and cohesion. Being in a group involves interaction, awareness of one another, relating to each another and some interdependence. The skill of winning involves the right attitude, quality performance, teamwork, a feeling of accountability to someone besides yourself, and a sense of competitiveness. It's a commitment to something bigger than yourself – a commitment to a team. You must lose any self-centered attitudes and become team-minded, playing not as an individual but as a unit. Teamwork is an attitude that you have to develop as a team and something you must be motivated to work on. Being a part of a team is a privilege not a right, you need to have respect for your sport and be committed to preparing to the best of your ability. Tom Seaver, "If you don't think baseball is a big deal, don't play it. But, if you do, play it right" (Dorfman & Kuehl, 1989, p. 46). Thinking in those terms, it becomes very clear, if you love your sport so much, have respect for it. Do everything in your power to showcase how spectacular the sport can be.

Your mind is always working, why not have it work for you? An athlete and a teams' strong will, determination and mental approach are of the greatest importance when it comes to how successful they will be in the heat of competition, and their ability to sustain their success over a long period of time. The reason a team plays great one day and bad the next can be explained in two words – **mental approach**. Their physical skills didn't change, but their mental approach did, which has a direct effect on the way they interact with one another. Since it seems that athletes use only a small fraction of their mental potential, it becomes obvious on the days when they are using those skills, and the days they are not, as stated by NBA player Charles Barkley, "... in the pros, one player is as good as another so you have to have a mental edge in order to reach your peak every night" (Barkley & Johnson, 1992, p. 147).

Athletes spend so much time physically practicing to get an edge on the competition. Yet, what a team can **really** do to get an edge is right in front of their nose, or more accurately, right above their shoulders! You hear the same thing all the time, "Sports is 90-95% mental." Athletes and coaches at all levels say it, but how many of them do something about it? Unfortunately, not nearly enough. It may be common knowledge, but it is not always common practice. Maybe they don't have the time, maybe they don't have the resources, or maybe down deep they don't really believe it. Whatever the reason, the fact remains the same, they are not utilizing their most powerful resource, the mind. Most athletes fatigue mentally before they fatigue physically, due to the fact that their mind is not in as good of shape as their bodies. Charles Barkley succinctly puts it, ". . . I learned the secret of NBA survival: conditioning of the body and mind" (Barkley & Johnson, p. 164).

The mind-body connection is a very powerful one. For everything you think in your mind, your body has a reaction, regardless of whether it is real or imagined. For example, have you ever had a bad dream? Usually, you will wake up and your heart is racing, you are sweating and very agitated, even though all you were doing was sleeping. But, in your mind there was something bad going on and your body was reacting to it. Here's another example: if you are home alone and you hear a noise and interpret it as the wind, you are fine; but if you interpret it as a prowler, your fight or flight response takes over and you become fearful, your heart begins going a mile a minute, your eyes dilate and you are scared. Another example is one in relation to ulcers. Ulcers are manifested through stress, worry and negative thoughts. The chemical imbalance allows enzymes to eat through the wall of your stomach, destroying the tissue, thus causing an ulcer (Curtis, 1989).

"You don't get ulcers from what you eat. You get them from what is eating you." Vicki Baum

These are just a few examples of how strong the connection is between your mind and your body. With this premise, it becomes unmistakable how necessary it is to train both the mind and body for peak performance.

It was very encouraging to see that, at the 1996 Summer Olympic Games in Atlanta, there were approximately 20 Sports Psychology Consultants there working with athletes. It has also been noted that 1/3 of the golfers on the major tours work with a Sports Psychologist or Consultant. Slowly but surely athletes, teams, coaches and managers are not only saying that they feel sports is mental, but they are doing something about it. They are hiring Sports Psychologists, reading books, and devoting time to team building and mental training. The way I look at it is this – in sports so, many things are left to chance; sports are predictably unpredictable – why let your mental mindset be another one of those things? There's no reason for your mental game to be your Achilles heel! You have the power and authority to control that. These tools and resources will help you remove psychological barriers that can get in the way of peak performance and give you some control over your own performance. Mark McGwire has worked with a Sports Psychologist since 1991, saying that the sessions help him find inner peace. He said it was totally his decision and the best one he made (Fernandez, 1994, A-10).

Up until about a decade ago, a Sports Psychologist or Consultant was considered a person who athletes went to see only when they had a problem, not someone who healthy and productive athletes and teams spent their time with. Luckily, this stigma is changing; the change is slow, but it is evident. You see Sports Psychologists everywhere now; recreational athletes, colleges, professional teams, Olympic athletes, businesses, and corporations all seek them out. People are realizing that no matter how good you are, you can always improve, and one way to improve yourself is to become well-versed in performance enhancement techniques. There is no room for complacency – the complacent ones get left behind. This philosophy holds true not only in sports but in business as well.

Competition is so tight, athletes are so physically fit, and the margin for victory so slim, that managers, coaches and players are realizing that to get ahead they need an added resource – and that resource is a trained mind. Yet still, many coaches are blind to how important the mental skills of their athletes really are. When there are two teams that are physically equal, it is the team that works together smoothly and is mentally prepared and confident that will come out on top. Keep in mind though, no mental training will compensate for ineffective technique. In *The Mental Game of Baseball*, Tom Seaver talks about the differences between the team that wins and the team that loses as, "the effort they give, the mental alertness that keeps them from making mental mistakes. The concentration and the dedication - the intangibles - are the deciding factors" (Dorfman & Kuehl, p. 1). You need to be strong, technically **and** mentally. Unfortunately, many times one aspect of your game is magnified at the expense of the other, instead of giving equal attention to both, which is the ideal approach. You are given the talent, it's your job to develop it and watch it flourish by combining physical and mental training with a great work ethic. Oklahoma State University's Baseball Coach Gary Ward says, "Combining the two elements gives the players an opportunity to establish a consistent, peak performance every time they step on the field" (Brennan, 1990, p. 252). You want your team to be prepared mentally and physically to the best of its' ability to increase the chance of success. It all comes down to Darwinism – survival of the fittest: learning the necessary skills to survive in your environment.

Now, here comes the tricky part. Even if all the athletes on the team are physically and mentally prepared, if they do not function as one unit, they can fall prey to the opposition. That is where this book comes into play. Because before you can work on performance enhancement skills such as relaxation, imagery, focusing, and confidence; you must first and foremost build a solid, working team. One that has a mission, common long and short-term goals in mind, a strong bond, excellent communication and good leadership. A team is much more than the sum of its parts. The dynamics within the group play a significant role in its' success.

This book provides practical tools to help teams gain awareness, control thoughts and behaviors and be prepared, both as individual players **and** as a team. The information is presented in an easy-to-understand format that can be applied immediately. It is based on research, personal experience and interviews. Most players, coaches and managers are eager to know how to build and maintain a sound, mentally tough team. The key is to establish the team, **then** teach the mental training skills. Mental training is a way of reprogramming the mind to achieve more positive behaviors and outcomes, capitalizing on your natural abilities to reach peak performance. This book doesn't put the cart before the horse by teaching the sports psychology skills and then leaving it to chance that the team will function well as a group. The objective is to provide information that educates you on the importance of team building and mental training; and to give strategies and techniques that will help your team reach the performance level desired. This book helps you build the team – **then** enhance it.

The first part of this book will be geared towards characteristics of peak performance, how groups are formed, and the stages it has to go through before it can start doing meaningful work. Then, defining what constitutes a cohesive group, how to achieve this and how to be a team player will be given a great deal of attention. The importance of leadership, effective communication and how to give and receive feedback properly will finish up this part.

Once a working group is established it can then go on to the performance enhancement techniques that can, and should, be applied to the individual athletes as well as the group as a whole. Topics such as motivation, mission statements, goal setting, relaxation, imagery, concentration, positive self-talk and confidence will be covered. All of these sport psychology techniques are interwoven, the development of one helps with the growth and proficiency of another. Just like with mathematics, you need to be proficient in adding and subtracting before moving on to multiplying and dividing, the same holds true here. You need to have the motivation before you can set goals. You need to be proficient in relaxation skills, before you move on to imagery, etc.

Unfortunately, there can be, and usually are, some hitches in sports. Nothing is guaranteed to be smooth sailing the whole time. Teams are going to face rough waters at times by means of choking, slumping, and dealing with an injury. That's why there is a section designated to trouble shooting some of the most common problems that athletes and teams may experience during the course of a season.

This book provides the strategies necessary for developing a solid foundation to help your team reach peak performance in any of its endeavors, be it in the board room or in the sporting arena. Keep in mind that these sports psychology skills are life skills as well, and can be applied to any undertaking – job, family, school, etc. A philosophy of sport is almost identical to a philosophy of life – a strong commitment to one aspect of your life will have a ripple effect into other areas of your life. You can use the skills to improve your "game" and to contribute more to the "team" you are a part of to produce the desired results.

"A sound mind in a sound body is a short but complete description of a happy life." John Locke, English Philosopher

Chapter 1
In The Zone

Before we actually started talking about team building and mental training, I feel it is important that we focus for a minute on what exactly it means to be "in the flow." Since this, ultimately, is where we want to be – performing at a peak level more times than not, and not just **by chance**. This chapter will examine some of the universal characteristics of that "best performance." This way you will have more control and awareness about these peak performances and they won't seem as mysterious as they once might have. Baseball player Gary Carter describes it this way, "I think I could come to home plate, stand on my head, and still get a hit when I'm feeling like this" (Dorfman & Kuehl, p. 24). That sense of invincibility is so vital because that complete confidence is what makes your body relaxed and your mind clear so that you **can** be in the flow.

In the flow, in a grove, on a roll, in the zone – whatever you call it, it's all defining one thing. It's that special feeling of playing like you can do no wrong and everything goes your way. You are so involved in what you are doing that nothing else seems to matter because you are so connected to your task. When former Boston Celtic star Bill Russell characterizes being in the zone he says it is, "a moment when everything goes so perfectly that you slip into a gear that you didn't even know was there" (Greider, 1991, p. 17). Unfortunately, this doesn't seem to happen enough of the time. In fact, every time it does happen, it is usually by chance; you took no real active part in it. It just happened to be a day when everything fell into place, clicked for you, and you got a taste of what it's like to be "in the zone." It's kind of like getting a taste of the good life. Hopefully this occurrence will motivate you to do everything you can to have more peak performances.

By implementing mental training skills and working effectively as a team, you can increase the chances of this transpiring on a more consistent basis and you will be able to be in the zone as one harmonious unit. The Japanese call it "satori" – the magical state where a player is completely focused on the task at hand, relaxed and mentally clear (Albinson & Bull, 1990). Being in the zone means doing more than anyone else thought possible, even superseding your own expectations at times. This zone is the definitive reason why many people are motivated to participate in sports.

Take a few minutes and think about a time when you were in the zone. As a player, it's the time when everything came together for you – it was exactly the kind of performance that you'd like to repeat over and over again. As a coach, it's the day when you were confident in all the plays you called, and again, everything just fell into place with minimal effort. There were no bad plays called or any second guessing as to what the "right" decision was – only a flow from beginning to end. When I was a competing as a skater, there was a parent in the rink who said it best. During practice, after a flawless routine she would say, "That's the one you want to put in your pocket and take with you to every competition." She summed it up perfectly! But, what exactly did that routine encompass that was so magical?

Exercise #1

Go back to that perfect routine, game, outing, whatever it was, and examine all aspects of it. Write down everything about it, be as detail-oriented as possible. Keep in mind the sequence of events, how you felt, and what the prominent characteristics were. Relive the event being as precise as you can; no detail is too small to mention. This is the starting point, finding out exactly what you want to be doing – and not leaving out a single detail. It is what you ultimately want to do as often as possible. After you've written it down, read this to yourself every day – reliving it each time.

"I'm in this quiet zone, I don't hear anything, and it enables me to use my inner peace and strength to go out and play," says San Francisco 49er Defensive Back Marquez Pope. Peak performers have a strong sense of mission, enjoy the challenge, have the ability to stay focused on the goals and have unwavering confidence in themselves. What sets them apart is their burning commitment to themselves, their teammates and their goals. Peak performers in any arena, business or sports, are devoted to doing the best job possible for themselves and for the people on their team.

Characteristics of being IN THE ZONE

1. **Relaxed** – The days of getting psyched up to play are over. Research has shown over and over that the best performances occur when you are just slightly above your normal state of arousal, not at the extreme end of the spectrum as once thought. You are energized, yet relaxed – it's a subtle balance of quiet intensity. Your mind is calm and your body is ready to go. You feel relaxed, but you are able to move with great strength and ease.

2. **Confident** – Not letting a lapse in performance undermine your belief in your overall abilities is at the core of this characteristic. When you are playing well, you feel confident that no matter what you are up against, you are going to come out on top. You just exude with confidence and pride, and it is evident in your performance. There is no fear. Confidence on the inside is outwardly shown by way of your presence, your walk and your facial expressions. You are completely self-assured and poised as you proceed through the game. You should **expect** to be successful, not hope or wish to be successful. You must adopt a confident, winning attitude.

   It is trusting your instincts and intuition to do the right thing at the right time; and if you are prepared, you can be confident that this will happen. This complete faith allows you to "just know" that you are going to do everything necessary to be successful without the conscious use of reasoning or analyzing. Gary Boren, Free Throw Therapist who works with the Golden State Warriors, says, "It's virtually an empty-headed shot ... you can only think about the target and trust your muscles" (Fernandez, p. A-11).
3. **Completely focused** – You are totally absorbed in the moment. You have no memory of the past and no qualms about the future; you are here now. The **only** thing you are concentrating on is the task at hand. You are oblivious to everything else going on around you – consumed by the moment. Like a child playing with his/her* toys, you are so absorbed in the moment that nothing outside can effect you. You have no real sense of time, and before you know it, the game is over. The game seems to have flown by, and at the same time, everything you did seemed to happen in a slowed-down pace with great precision and

concentration. Having the ability to stay in the moment is a gift that all of peak performers have. Recently, I was working with a Division I Collegiate Women's Volleyball team and they were describing a match they had played a few days earlier. One of the girls mentioned that once she stepped out onto the court, she didn't hear or see anything that wasn't game-related and that she had "tunnel vision"; the player next to her said, "you were in the zone."

4. **Effortless** – Things just sort of happen with little or no effort whatsoever. All your moves are smooth and for that time, volleyball, football, baseball, basketball, whatever it may be, seems like the easiest thing in the world. You are in a state of mind and body where you can accomplish great things with little effort. In *USA Weekend*, U.S. Rower Jon Brown says, "You get into this magical feel ... Everything is in sync, you're making the boat move fast, but it feels effortless" (McNichol, 1996, p. 5). Your mind and body are working with one another in perfect unison. The grace and ease that you display make everything you do seem like the simplest task in the world. You have a sense of finesse and grace, even when the task is very grueling and demanding. That sort of connectedness and moment of greatness is an awesome thing to both witness and take part in.
5. **Automatic** – There is no interference from your thoughts or emotions. Things are just happening, both without protest and without consent. You are on auto pilot – just reacting to whatever comes your way. Your body just seems to know what to do without any directive from you. There is no conscious thought involved; you're going strictly on your instincts. "A good athlete can enter a state of body awareness in which the right stroke or right movement happens by

itself, effortlessly" (Mitchell, 1988, p. viii). If you think less, you will achieve more.

6. **Fun** – When you're in the flow, the enjoyment is incomparable to anything else. You feel like when you were a kid enjoying your sport with pure and innocent delight. Anyone can see in your eyes the satisfaction and fulfillment the sport gives you. You feel like your sport is giving you back something that you can't get from anyone or anything else. This is a key factor because if you don't enjoy your sport, your future in it will be limited.
7. **In Control** – You feel that no matter what, you are in control. What you think and want to happen will. You have ultimate command over your emotions as well – you are controlling them, not the other way around. When you are in control, you are in charge. You govern your own destiny. When you feel this strong of a command over your game, great things are sure to happen. The authority is yours, and no one else's.

   Bill Bradley talks about taking command and being in control when he speaks of a game his team (Knicks) played against the Milwaukee Bucks and were down by 19 points with 5 minutes to go, "Suddenly we 'caught fire'. Everything we shot went in... We won by three points, accomplishing what came to be known as a 'believer feat.' Those who saw it believed our invincibility, I even think we did" (Bradley, 1976, p. 92).

Chungliang Al Huang states, "Sport is a whole brain and body activity. To be good in sport requires the presence and participation of your mind, body and spirit in total synchronization" (Huang & Lynch, 1992, p. xxi). I think this is worth restating – **your mind, body and spirit have to be working together to be successful**. And, this usually encompasses the characteristics that we just talked about. After looking at these, if you go back to the time when you were in the flow, I'm sure you will be able to put a check next to some of the qualities mentioned above.

Mental Toughness

Another phrase you often hear when people are talking about peak performance is being **mentally tough**. Being mentally tough is the ability to encompass all these characteristics, at the same time, no matter what the situation is, on a consistent basis. Your internal feelings and approach doesn't change just because the circumstances do. The ability to bounce back positively after adversity (i.e., a lost game, interception, strike out) with great composure can make all the difference in the world. Games can be won or lost in a matter of seconds. A mentally tough athlete responds to adversity with technique, not emotion. In sports and in life, as the pressure increases, your most deep-rooted personal characteristics become evident. So, those characteristics had better be ones that are conducive to peak performance and handling adversity well!

The mentally tough athlete is serious about the goals he has chosen, and pursues them with such a persistence, that many people would call him stubborn. But, that strong determination to succeed tends to supersede anything that could be a potential obstacle to most other athletes. Having that fighting spirit in any and all situations is one of your most powerful resources. "Persistence can overshadow talent as the most valued and effective resource in shaping your quality of life" (Robbins, 1991, p. 299). That fire to push through any circumstance must be evident, and **is** apparent in all the best athletes. This athlete makes good choices and takes responsibility for his actions, realizing that his behavior is a function of his decisions. He has control and balance in all aspects of his game and life. If this balance isn't present then there will be a breakdown, either mentally or physically. "A mentally tough player is a self-motivated player with a desire to succeed as his focus," says Gary Ward, Oklahoma State University Head Baseball Coach (Brennan, p. 253).

Mental toughness is what separates good teams from great teams. Great teams like the challenge and are committed to excellence in all areas of life and come through in clutch situations due to discipline and control – they never panic. The collective confidence of the team remains intact, even when mistakes are made. They are never intimidated. They pull together during times of tribulation and have the composure to draw their resources together and come out a winner. There are no peaks and valleys, just an even-keeled approach. Good teams do well under normal circumstances, but it becomes a toss-up in clutch situations. **It's time to become a great team.**

Sounds like a tall order, but with hard work and discipline it can be done. It is a learned state, one that can be developed – starting here, starting now. Mental toughness is a skill you can acquire, by being prepared and mentally sound in every situation. You can build mental strength through repetition, just as you do physical strength. Peak performers know this and abide by it. Many athletes tell me that they just turn "it" on during games; they don't concern themselves that much with being committed to their mental game during practice. They say they are just "game players." I'm not quite sure what that means, but I do know that if you aren't committed to your practice and preparation, there won't be anything to "turn on" come game day. Saying your a "gamer" interferes with your conditioning because there is a lack of consistency and accountability, which shows on game day. In some cases, games are won or lost before the first play due to pregame preparation, or lack thereof. Peak performer, San Francisco 49er Marquez Pope says, "I use the same techniques through the week and game so there is no change. The way I am on the practice field is the way I want to be in the game. So, if I do mess up I know why and I don't throw in a lot of different moves."

Talent will only get you so far, you have to possess mental toughness and a strong character to get you where you want to go and to help keep you there. Sports has demonstrated many times how the team with commitment, character and mental toughness can win over a team with a **seemingly** more physically talented group. This fact alone shows you how important character and mental toughness are. "The mental make-up of an athlete is huge - it's incredible. I've seen athletes with a lot of talent, but they can't make it from Triple A to the big leagues, because emotionally they can't deal with it," says Sports Attorney Rockne Lucia, Jr.

Commitment

Now that we know some of the characteristics surrounding peak performance, it's important to talk about commitment. I think a good place to start is with practice. One missed practice, one day with only 50% effort can too quickly become a habit. If you're committed to your game, you're also committed to your training. You have to be devoted to all of it, not just the easy part.

"The will to win is important, the will to prepare is vital."
Joe Paterno

This can often times be the difference between being successful or not, especially when the margin of victory is so small. You must have a strong burning commitment to your goals and aspirations, in this lies the key. Because it is this that will keep you going – knowing that you won't settle for less.

So many times you see athletes only practicing the things that they are already proficient at. The committed athlete knows that he has to push hard when it comes to the things that are difficult for him and turn those weaknesses into strengths. Nobody hands you excellence on a silver platter. You earn it through preparing and persisting in the face of all obstacles. Obstacles are new challenges, not walls to stop you. You need to understand that your commitment to your mental game will pay off big, if it is something you work hard at every day, just like your physical skills. You must persist through the discomfort of adding something new to your training, and realize that it can help you reach the goals you have set for yourself. Quality physical practice **and** mental practice, combined, lead to better performances.

"Man cannot discover new oceans unless he has the courage to lose sight of the shore." André Gide

If it's what you strongly desire you have to stay committed. No matter what anyone else says or thinks about it. I'm sure we can all relate to this: In one endeavor or another in our lives there will always be at least one person who will have their doubts about your ability. It's up to you to not listen. Let it go in one ear and out the other. If it is what you truly want, make the decision to go for it 100% and be persistent in your endeavors. "Making a true decision means committing to achieving a result, and then cutting yourself off from any other possibility" (Robbins, 1991, p. 39). So it then becomes a matter of **when** you will achieve it, not **if** you are going to achieve it!

One way to keep yourself committed, is to be aware of your own style of backsliding; for example, you know that your commitment is being challenged when you find yourself making excuses so you can go out with your friends rather than practice. Or, you chose to not practice today, and feel you will make it up tomorrow. You **must** be committed all the time. One way to help ensure this is to have the attitude that success is process you want to continue, not a status you reach once and for all. Having the latter attitude can lead to complacency. Remember, preparation is a 365-day thing, there's always room for improvement. San Francisco 49er Steve Young had this to say about teammate Jerry Rice, "I want kids to understand that no matter how great you are, you don't get better unless you work hard. He's the greatest of all time because of his work ethic" (Crumpacker, 1994, p. C-1). What you do in the off season and the pre-season will set the tone for the entire season; this in turn sets the stage for your entire career. By having a consistent approach all year long, you increase your probability of doing well and succeeding.

Success in not a matter of chance, it's a matter of decision, commitment and a pursuit of knowledge. Your performance level is strongly correlated to your commitment. Winning will be a by-product of your determination, desire and commitment to mental and physical preparation. It's not just your abilities that will determine your success, but your **ability to prioritize**. You need to be a conscientious worker and act in accordance with what you know makes great performers. We all have this knowledge, yet at times we choose to ignore it instead of having an open mind to methods of improving. You want to direct your behavior in ways that you can raise your head high and feel proud of yourself.

"Where there is an open mind, there will always be a frontier." Charles F. Kettering

In summary, we have taken some time to discuss what characteristics are encompassed in peak performances. They are things we all have experienced, just not always all at once! The exercise completed in this chapter is going to be a yardstick as you improve and grow – keep it close by. Strive to be a mentally tough player, one whose approach never changes, no matter what. And finally – commitment, commitment, commitment. You've taken your first step by getting this far in the book, just take the next step (Chapter 2), and the next (Chapter 3) and so on.

* From this point forward I will use he when referring to either he or she for the sake of simplicity.

Chapter 2
Getting it together

I'm sure many of you have heard the acronym TEAM - Together Everyone Achieves More. Well, before this can come to fruition the team has to be built and bond to the point that it **can** "achieve more." This chapter will address how a team is formed, the stages of development it will go through and what it means to be a sound team player and how crucial your individual contributions are.

What constitutes a team?

Groups never come into being without a purpose. People join together in all walks of life to accomplish a common goal - knowing that together they can make great things happen. The success of any organization will depend upon individual abilities and how skillful the team is at solving problems. Just as important is the ability of the group to act as one unit on a consistent basis. A team will be successful only if it does the right thing at the appropriate time. Group success is the collective achievement of a team working as one to achieve a specific goal or objective.

A team is a group of people who have norms that regulate their behavior to some degree. They each have a role that is interdependent with the other members of the team. Teams differ from a collection of individuals in many ways. Teams have members who can talk freely about things that not only relate to the group, but also about things that are happening on or off the field/court that may be affecting their productivity. They have agreed-upon goals, are genuinely concerned about achieving these goals as a group, and in turn, are mutually helpful. Teams are interested in the welfare of its members and are willing to assist their teammates. Team members use terms such as "we" and "they" and participate wholeheartedly. They have a shared language that only they can interpret, whereas a collection of individuals probably won't have this. There is also loyalty among members that keeps them persistent during hard times, rather than just giving up because there is a struggle. A sense of loyalty will help align all the members.

I think we can conclude that a team is a group of people who share common goals, a common vision and have some level of interdependence that requires both verbal and physical interaction. Teams come into existence through shared attitudes. They may come together for a number of different reasons, but their goals are the same – to achieve peak performance in their endeavors. Only the way it is measured differs; one might make the conclusion based on sales increases, another by having the best record in the NBA. The ends may differ but the means by which one gets there is the same. And it all starts with one thing – building a sound, working team.

Group Formation

"Coming together is a beginning; keeping together is progress; and working together is success." Henry Ford

Teams evolve over a period of time. Groups go through the process of forming, storming, norming, and performing in its development (Tuckman, 1965). These stages may overlap and some things may take place during a different stage than is mentioned here, this is a general guideline. During the initial stage of forming there are certain things that will most likely take place:

- ✔ Members are getting acquainted – Players are learning something new each day about the members of this team and getting acclimated to their new environment. They are finding out who plays which position, who hangs around with who, the strengths of their teammates, etc.
- ✔ Some resistance – Certain members may not like specific aspects of the way the particular program is run at the beginning, and will try to resist conforming as long as possible. Some might also resist the hierarchy that they are facing. For example, they were at the higher end of the hierarchy in high school, and find themselves at the lower end as a freshman in college. Once a big fish in a small pond, now a small fish in a big pond!
- ✔ Testing the waters/boundaries – The athletes want to see if they'll be taken seriously and how far they can take things. For example, is the coach as strict as he says? Will I get reprimanded for certain behaviors? Do I have to show up 10 minutes early for **every** team meeting?
- ✔ Learning how the group functions – No two teams are the same, so no matter how many different teams a player has been on, there will still be a lot to learn about **this** particular team. Whether this is the 10th team a player has been on or the first, there is still the same amount to learn about **this** team.
- ✔ Dealing with this awkward time – Members are expressing both positive and negative feelings about the group. Players tend to look to others to see what is acceptable, since at this stage there is a lack of

clarity and most don't want to ruffle any feathers. This lack of clarity can make many uncomfortable.

- ✔ The player's talents and abilities are scrutinized – At this time their position on the team is either secured or upset. Joining a team brings with it a degree of risk and can put players in a vulnerable position during this period.
- ✔ The goals, roles, responsibilities and objectives of the team are made clear – Ideally, this should be done at an initial team meeting. It is also beneficial to have an individual meeting with each member to go over rules and responsibilities surrounding their assigned role. Goals must be explicitly stated, understood and accepted by the members early on. Otherwise conflict, confusion and fragmentation could occur at a later date.

Storming is the transition stage. Once the players decide this is where they want to be, it doesn't mean smooth sailing from there on out (unfortunately). During this stage, structure may be resisted or challenged while each member is learning to work with differences.

"We didn't all come over in the same ship, but here we are in the same boat." Unknown

Some of the attributes of this stage are:

- ✔ Anxiety – There is a fear of looking foolish, stepping out of roles that are familiar to them, being misunderstood and rejected. For example, a converted 3rd baseman from 1st base may be anxious that his talents may not be given the appropriate attention since he is not displaying his normal ease and proficiency at this point with the position. If they are now playing at a higher level (going from being a college star to a rookie on a professional team) they may be anxious and unsure how to handle this newfound awkwardness.

- ✔ Defensiveness and resistance – Players may become defensive of their opinions about the way certain things should be done, or what they have been used to in the past on other teams. For instance, saying that your last coach didn't see anything wrong with the way you threw, or that on your last team players didn't have to condition early in the morning. Put your ego and uncertainties aside and respect the way things are done on this present team.
- ✔ Struggle for control – Behaviors including rivalry, jealousy, competing for positions, and discussions about division of responsibility may be apparent here. Older players may try to pawn things off on the new players because of seniority. "Blue chip" athletes may feel they have more of a say because of their abilities and are exempt from certain things.
- ✔ Conflict with members or coaches – If the conflict is handled correctly trust will increase, if it is not addressed it can be quite destructive. Many times, venting feelings is a way of testing trustworthiness of the group. Trust takes time to develop and is very easy to lose. So it's important to do everything you can to maintain and nurture that trust once it is developed. Unresolved issues tend to come back and bite the team at a later date or manifest themselves by way of resentment by certain members. Resentment then eats away at the team's togetherness. Conflict, many times, is a result of miscommunication or misinterpretation of team standards, roles, norms and goals (Vernacchi, 1992).
- ✔ Conflict is a healthy part of the group's process – Conflict resolution methods must be explored to see how the group can best deal with conflict. Once all

this has taken place, the group can begin to function as a team. Many times, conflict can force the group to become cohesive quicker. I'm sure you've heard stories about how a team had to go through some conflict or adversity early on and then the group's bond was that much stronger in a shorter period of time. The members and the team have to be resilient to any changes resulting from the conflict.

- ✔ Dealing with conflict – To successfully deal with conflict you need to: acknowledge it, identify common ground, seek to understand all angles of conflict, and not attack one another. Then, develop a written action plan that's agreed upon that will help resolve this conflict and hopefully reduce the chances of it happening again. There must be a willingness to deal with it and then move on without holding any grudges or carrying any baggage from the conflict.
- ✔ Conflict resolution – Successful resolution results in an increase in self-esteem, respect, trust, and decision-making skills. All of which encourage the development of a close-knit, resourceful team. Once the conflict has been resolved all the members can move forward. They reach a new level of respect and acceptance. There is great satisfaction knowing that you worked through a problem successfully as a team.

The third stage is norming. This is where cohesion begins to develop, norms are formed and trust increases. Teams will now begin to establish social norms which will regulate the behavior of all the members.

- ✔ Norms – Norms reflect a team's consensus about what the acceptable and unacceptable behaviors are. Group norms are the shared beliefs about expected behaviors that are geared toward making the team function effectively (Corey & Corey, 1987). The values and rules must be accepted by all that plan to be a part of the team. The rules are put in place to help keep the team running smoothly and systematically in order to meet the goals. If no norms are established the team's habits (good or bad) will become the norm by way of default and lack of structure (Fisher, 1995). Many times, having players sign a contract with the rules, and consequences if they are broken, can have a positive effect on the team. Rules are designed to provide focus and consistency among team members.

✔ Expectations – Players need to know what is expected of them to aid them in reaching their goals and objectives. There can be no gray areas, everything must be spelled out (i.e., expected to attend practice/meetings regularly, basic operating procedures, how information is relayed, travel attire, customary standards of behavior, etc.). These norms set the tone for the whole season. It is important that everyone accept these so the team can work harmoniously. If group norms are clearly presented and the players see the value of them, then these norms will be powerful forces in shaping the group. It's harder to go back and change a norm than it is to establish practical ones at the beginning of the season. There will be enough outside obstacles for the team to contend with, so there is no need to create unnecessary chaos within the team due to something that is under their control to take care of at the beginning of the season. Having clear group expectations is important in determining whether cohesion will be effectively developed, which in turn will directly effect the team's performance.

- ✔ Members are able to give feedback freely - This feedback is accepted with a willingness to reflect on its accuracy and to see someone else's point of view. The team members know that it is given with the design to help the individual and the group. This feedback should be taken in a positive manner, knowing the intention behind it is a good one. They now feel comfortable that they can openly give input and express opinions.
- ✔ Teamwork - Teamwork becomes evident in this stage as team members openly support and encourage one another. Napoleon Hill said, "Teamwork is a neverending process, and even though it depends on everyone involved, the responsibility for it lies with you" (Sartwell, 1994, p. 149). Every member of the team is accountable when it comes to teamwork.

"You can achieve through the encouragement of others. ... Kindness and gentleness in your relations bring allegiance, cooperation and, ultimately, success." I Ching no. 58

Everyone involved needs to combine their efforts to succeed at the task at hand. If everyone does their job well, it increases what the team can accomplish. This teamwork has to be recognized by everyone; and know that great things can happen if individuals master the fundamentals and work together as one unit.

Teamwork is something that must be a high priority and given constant daily attention – it is not something that is achieved once and for all. Every player needs to understand how important it is for them to work smoothly together if they want to achieve their goals. You must be dedicated to the whole team and be willing to act unselfishly. When challenges arise, the team needs to have the resources, accountability and commitment to deal with them in a constructive manner – and teamwork plays an integral part in this. "When teams work, they represent the best proven way to convert embryonic visions and values into consistent action patterns because they rely on people working together" (Katzenbach & Smith, 1993, p. 19). It is amazing how much can be accomplished when no one cares who gets the credit!

A team is formed, it's members are in place, a trusting environment is beginning to be established, and cooperative behaviors are encouraged in an effort to attain team success. The members have now decided that they are going to be a part of this group and want the team to be proficient. The foundation has been set for the team to move on to its next stage.

Performing now becomes the working, or flow, stage. Here is where the group's structure, purpose and roles all come together so they can function as one. Some of the things that become evident in this final stage are as follows:

- ✔ The commitment and attention that the members give to the dynamics of the group is quite noticeable in this stage. They realize and appreciate what it has taken to get to this point and are able to look back and see how far they have come. They now consider themselves as part of something bigger and are eager to see their hard work pay off.
- ✔ The members discover the universality of the team. The group is composed of many different people, but as the team become more cohesive these differences aren't focused on as much as the universality of purpose. Here is where the "lightbulb goes on" and they see why they have gone through everything they

have up to this point and where it can lead them. They rise above their differences and focus on common ground. This bonding allows the group to move forward. Members use one another as a resource and have an awareness of group process and what makes the team productive/unproductive. "Nearly all successful people have in common an extraordinary ability to bond with people from a variety of backgrounds and beliefs" (Robbins, 1986, p. 32).

- ✔ The players should have a clear understanding of their role, purpose, boundaries and resources. They realize the importance of these things to the success of their team. With everyone working within their defined role and with their purpose in mind they are more apt to see positive results. When there is role conflict or ambiguity this can lead to dissatisfaction and ill feelings on the team. So, it is very important that by this stage everyone have a crystal clear picture of what is expected of them.
- ✔ Genuine cohesion typically can be seen in this stage after groups have struggled with conflict, shared pain, and have committed themselves to taking risks by trusting and opening up to one another. This usually takes place after the storming phase and shows itself in this stage. Some indicators are a willingness to be punctual and showing support for others. There seems to be an unspoken understanding among the players and here is where everything can visibly come together. According to Yalom (1983), groups having a here-and-now focus are almost invariably vital and cohesive. Through this process a climate for the team to feel free do meaningful work is produced.

Team Image

Having a common group identification definitely lends itself to the productivity of the team. Group identity is determined by the knowledge, strength, and significance of a player's membership on a particular team (Murrell & Gaertner, 1992). Teams must be similar in attitude and level of commitment. Having one group identity, rather than being divided into a number of subgroups or cliques, is associated with successful team performance. If you feel that you are a part of a group, you are usually more motivated to do worthwhile work and help enhance the team. Teams stimulate individuals to higher performance levels. If you choose to not work together or just stick to superficial interactions, there won't be as much team togetherness, and division among them will occur (Corey, & Corey). Having an "every man for himself" mentality will cause a split among the players.

"A house divided against itself cannot stand." Abraham Lincoln

Subgroups may not only have an effect on the overall positive atmosphere, but also may hinder the formation of a collective team identity, which in turn might interfere with successful team performance (Murrell & Gaertner). Fragmentation and cliques will also undermine, instead of enhance, the level of respect among team members. Negative subgroups will work against, not with, the rest of the team. Teams need to feel like one unit, not a group of individuals or subgroups.

Making sure that the team's image is a positive one is integral. Each team functions within the image it has of itself – this is referred to as a self-fulfilling prophecy. If the team has the attitude that they are a confident and aggressive team, then they will portray that image on the outside by the way they carry themselves, and the way they feel about themselves on the inside. The team gets its image by way of uniforms/colors, mascot, team slogans, formations/rituals, and the interplay of the members. Gathering the team together before taking the field/court to call upon your slogan can help bond the team and enhance its' confidence before entering the game. "We are the Tigers," symbolizing you are inseparable, unbeatable, aggressive and ready to go. Rituals and traditions create a strong spirit of unity among team members. "Everybody that's drafted here knows that they come here with one thing in mind, and that's to uphold the tradition we've had over the last 15 years, and that's to win with class, work hard and to set standards for themselves that go out to the rest of the league and the media," says San Francisco 49ers Owner Eddie DeBartolo, Jr. This is how a team takes the appropriate action to produce results. Encouraging a group to have one identity can help make a team closer. Through this they can develop pride and confidence in their team. That team pride can create an unmistakable arrogance on the playing field that provides you with a definite edge. Your presence is known as soon as you arrive.

When there is a negative team image, the team will play in accordance with that image as well, whether it be an image they have created or one that was bestowed upon them by the media, other teams, fans, etc. The team then needs to do things to help change this negative image. This can be done by creating new positive slogans, changing their outward appearance (uniforms, body language, how vocal they are), and the rituals they take part in. Also, when a team culture is not adequately developed, then the team will function below its capabilities. A team has to be flexible and realize when things aren't working or when they are counterproductive. Dr. Jamie Williams, former Tight End for the San Francisco 49ers, says, "There's a shared culture. When you come to your orientation they let you know what is important to the 49ers, what is the goal of the 49ers, what is the vision of the 49ers, what they tolerate and what they don't tolerate."

Exercise #2

Ask your players (or teammates) what image they want to portray. What characteristics do you (as a team) want to possess? Where are we now? When other teams look at us what do they see? This provides an opportunity for players to take a good, hard look at themselves as a team and can provide an incentive to change certain things.

Team Harmony

Team harmony effects everything - motivation for training, openness to learning, commitment to improving performance, feelings of personal acceptance, and overall satisfaction with the quality of interpersonal relationships between players and coaches. Only once a team is well synchronized can it draw the most from the strengths and abilities of its' individual members. You have to feed off of each other's strong points so the team will be more productive. Each of you should be aware of how you fit into the whole picture. What you achieve as a team will most likely be more satisfying than anything you achieve on your own - you can't win a conference title on your own, the World Series, the Super Bowl, or become CEO of a major corporation. No matter how valuable you are to the team, you are not the sole cause of a team win or loss. Team knowledge **always** exceeds any one individual's knowledge. This harmony creates a strong bond among the team both on and off the field, and this is vital to the success of the team.

Chinese Philosopher Sun Tzu (1963) says that, "National unity was deemed to be an essential requirement of victorious war" (p. 39). You can't win the war unless you are sure you are all on the same team and fighting for the same thing! As a team, there must be discipline and unity, otherwise your team will always come up short. You are voluntarily combining your efforts and then trusting the outcome. You must have confidence in your teammates to perform well and act in the best interest of the team. Keep in mind, that doing something good for the team, will more than likely be beneficial to you as well. When the team wins, you win. An example of this is if a pitcher has complete trust in his catcher, that will free his mind to concentrate solely on throwing; which will more than likely result in a more effective performance by the pitcher. Or, if a quarterback has complete trust in his offensive line then he can focus on getting the ball to an open receiver. “If everybody competes against their own opponent and works to win, then that brings a win for the whole team,” says San Francisco 49er Defensive Back Marquez Pope.

It’s also important to have good team morale. Morale is the team’s state of mind with respect to confidence, courage and discipline, and this is developed through team togetherness. Each member must be aware of the morale it is trying to maintain. “It is of great importance that the need for creating unity is recognized. The human spirit is nourished by a sense of connectedness.” I Ching no. 8

The harmony needs to stay intact regardless of what the team is going through. Many times when things are not going well the need to blame someone arises. Players come down on their teammates and/or coaches, feeling that maybe they did not do everything they should have. When things aren't going well that is the time to really depend on the harmony and unity among the team to help get through any troubling times. Napoleon Hill stated, "Two or more minds, united behind a definite major purpose and working in harmony to achieve it, will accomplish great things" (Sartwell, p. 10).

Having the right attitude is crucial in building a great team. You have to **want** to be there, and be motivated in the right direction. You need to be aware that commitment sometimes means sacrifice for the greater good. As Bill Bradley stated, "That is the beautiful heart of the game, the blending of personalities, the mutual sacrifices for group success" (Bradley, p. 157). Your teammates will sense if you aren't committed or you have a bad attitude. You must be genuinely dedicated physically and mentally to doing everything you can to maintain the harmony on the team.

When there is lack of team spirit or unity one way to handle this is to have a team meeting. In the meeting, have each player express what is hindering the team unity and give an example of a way it might be improved. The environment should be informal and comfortable for the players. It's also important for the coaches to stay positive, enthusiastic and to be consistent with team decisions so the players can stayed focused and positive as well.

Team Player

"1 man practicing sportsmanship is far better than 50 preaching it." Knute K. Rockne

Each of you has a choice to be on a team. Once you do choose to be a part of a team, there are still more choices to be made. You can choose to disclose when something is bothering you so that it can be resolved in an appropriate and timely manner, or you can choose to keep it to yourself, in which case no one benefits – you or the team.

You can be honest with yourself and your teammates about your thoughts and needs; or you can resort to game playing, saying and doing what you feel is expected of you and manipulating situations. You can choose to be cohesive with team members and work to develop a unifying bond, or you can choose to stay at a relationship born out of necessity that can result in fragmentation. Resentments that you only tell teammates and not the coach are a drain on the team, and can further break the club down. You can choose to take responsibility for your behavior (good and bad), or blame other players, coaches, family, equipment, officials, etc.

All of these choices come down to one thing – are you willing to be a team player or are you going to be an "I guy"? As a team player you must be aware of the team's overall mission and objectives and be sensitive to the needs of your teammates. There must be a willingness to listen to what your teammates and coaches are telling you and to work hard and be disciplined for not only yourself but also for the good of the team as a whole. The result of you being a team player or not, comes from the choices you make and the path you decide to take. Human choice is a gift and should be used constructively.

Being a sound team player is important, this isn't the only team you'll be a part of. There will be others – a family is a team, the job you choose will entail being a team member, and all corporations are teams. You need to get used to being part of a team and learn how to be a great team player so that it's a successful experience for everyone. This is good practice to get into, it will assist you in all parts of your life. "When you work in a law office, accounting office or anything else, you need to be able to deal with a team, with people, you've got to have interpersonal skills," says Sports Attorney Rockne Lucia, Jr. Never say, "that's not my job" when asked to do something; everyone has to help pick up the slack. You must be willing to work outside your defined role when asked. Great teams are cross-functional by design, players may have primary and secondary roles (Robbins & Finley, 1995). Successful teams are proud of what they have achieved and attribute it to hard work and dedication by everyone involved. Great team players are active, keep the game level high, know how to get the job done; they are energetic, enthusiastic and accountable – and these things are contagious.

This unselfish effort to help the group produces more than camaraderie and some wins. It helps you become a better athlete and allows everyone to perform at an optimal level on a more constant basis. Selflessness creates peace and conserves energy, which allows for higher levels of play for each of the members. We saw that happen at the 1996 Summer Olympic Games in Atlanta with Kerri Strug. She put the achievement of her team at the top of her priority list and "took one for the team" so to speak. She knew what had to be done so that she and her team could have a chance at winning the gold and she went out and did it. Bunting is also a good example of being unselfish and a team player. A lot of players would rather swing the bat than be told to bunt. But they put aside what they would prefer, and do what is best for the team in that particular situation. The more you can contribute to the team, the more valuable of a player you will be.

Another example, one that Pat Riley (1993) mentioned in *The Winner Within*, is that through Magic Johnson's unselfishness on the court he enhanced the skills of his teammates. He would draw defenders and then pass to whoever was open. No matter how good you are, no one individual can carry the team. You have to work together. You need to be an unselfish player and always keep in mind what is best for the team.

Giving to your teammates enhances your own performance in two ways – you're honing your own skills as a team player; and, teammates will usually reciprocate when the opportunity presents itself. You, more often then not, get something when you give to someone else. You are strengthening the bond between the members, and increasing the confidence you have in yourself as well as the confidence your teammates have in you. Helping and giving are just as important as receiving when you're talking about being a team player. "Teams reinforce each other's intention to pursue their team purpose above and beyond individual or functional agendas" (Katzenbach & Smith, p. 18). Developing good rapport between teammates requires that you be friendly, encourage each other, ask teammates for help when necessary, and tell them when you appreciate their help.

Individual contributions

Is there an "I" in team? To some people's surprise, the answer is yes. Some players are taught to focus **only** on team goals and outcomes and to lose themselves completely for the sake of the team. But research shows that the best performances, from individuals and groups, are when individual contributions are recognized as well as reinforced by teammates and coaches (Gill, 1986). Incentives such as "player of the week" and "game MVP" are examples of social stimuli that help keep motivation up. One of the deepest urges people have is the desire to feel important. When players are not credited or validated for their effort, they tend to lose motivation and slack off. Research by Jones (1974) compared team performance to individual statistics and found that group productivity was positively related to individual effectiveness.

Each individual must be made to feel important, and as a result, his sense of belonging and contribution to the team will increase. If every player adopts the attitude that if they step up it will make a difference, then the team can accomplish great things. It can be terrible when an individual athlete seems to have lost himself completely in the team. He doesn't really have his own identify anymore, he thinks only in terms of the team and has begun to base his own self-worth on the abilities of the team as a whole.

There must be regard for the individual talents and abilities of each team member. The special talents and achievements of individuals need to combine to function within a larger context. The role of each player both enrich and limit, but that does not take away from the fact that everyone is vital to the success of the team. Each carries out a role in relation to the other team members, and everyone makes a difference by way of his contributions. A player may not like the role he has been given, but if he understands the reasoning behind it he will more likely accept it and contribute to the team. Keep in mind that a weakness in one, weakens you all. If one athlete panics, it will affect the attitude of the whole team. On the same note, a team's collective thoughts will effect the collective outcome of their efforts.

Nonstarters

Many times nonstarters feel they are not valued by team members and the coaching staff. If some players feel alienated by other members, this may have a negative effect on the atmosphere of the team. Just because you aren't a starter doesn't make you any less part of the team. Getting frustrated with the coach or other members doesn't do anyone any good. You just need to be patient and work hard. You should practice with the motivation that once you do get a chance you are going to be ready to showcase your talents. That's what makes certain teams so great, when their starter goes down, the player taking his place is just as effective. The team that is out there is expected to do the job; no matter what, that team is the **present team**. There are no signs on you're back saying "I'm second string" or "This is my first start." And, while you're waiting for your turn, be a good team player, don't underestimate the importance of your support on the sidelines. Strive to be a key player and be constructive in some way on every team you are on.

It is not uncommon for nonstarters to have a little animosity and jealously towards those players that are always in the game, especially if they feel they could be playing equally as well, if not better, than those actually playing. You need to step back and see if the coach is doing what he thinks is best for the team as a whole, and have respect for what the coach decides. You also need to realize that when all is said and done, you are all on the same team with the same goal in mind – success. It's not good for all the nonstarters to have their own subgroup, this could lead to many problems. You need to stay interactive with all the members.

FOR COACHES: The way for coaches to approach nonstarters to keep them feeling a part of the team is to make an extra effort to praise good attributes, practice behavior, and contribution to team morale. This builds trust and commitment among the members. The attention will be greatly appreciated by the players and will motivate them to keep up what they are doing. If they feel the system and the coaches are fair, they can feel confident that they'll be given a chance when the time is right.

Team Interaction

All players must interact constantly, consistently, and effectively to be successful. They must integrate their individual skills to accomplish the group task. The smoother they are able to synchronize their tasks, the more successful the team will be. The success is likely to be explained by an attitude of "We are the team to beat tonight." The way team members interact will play a huge role in relation to their effectiveness and success. They must work together so that their energy is directed towards maximizing their talents.

Although it may seem logical that the team with the best individual athletes will make up the best team, this is not always the case. Success is not simply the sum of individual talent, and just because you have the most talented athletes on the team doesn't mean you will win all the games. United States Olympic Rower Doug Burden says, "You don't necessarily want the fastest 8 guys. You want the guys who work best together." (McNichol, p. 5). Although, team success does have a great deal to do with the individual abilities of the team members. However, developing a team concentrating solely on the training of individuals is as inappropriate as trying to predict a team's performance by simply adding individual talents and comparing them to their opponent's talents. The missing elements in such a prediction are the dynamics and relationships within the team, which can make or break a team during the heat of competition (Freischlag, 1985). There has to be an interplay and a willingness of all the members of the team to work together. A team or organization will achieve results based on two things – the knowledge and skills of the individuals involved **and** their ability to work together as one unit.

The whole must be greater than the sum of its parts. Interaction becomes more complex as the number of individuals within a group increases. As groups increase in size there is a diffusion of responsibility among members. Steiner's Group Productivity Model (1972) says that actual productivity equals potential productivity minus losses due to faulty process. Potential productivity is a team's best possible performance given its resources, and as resources increase, so does potential productivity. So it follows suit that having highly-skilled players makes for greater resources. Faulty processes come by way of motivation and coordination losses (Williams & Widmeyer, 1991). Examples of coordination losses are poor timing, bad strategy, bad throw, and miscommunication on plays. Motivation losses are things such as slacking off and giving less than 100 percent. With this premise, the more connected a group is the more likely they will communicate, practice, have a greater commitment to the goal; and therefore, will increase the quality of their performance. The stronger the need for coordination and cooperation in a given sport, the greater the chances that a strong bond will reduce a decrease in productivity due to coordination losses. A team's strengths and weaknesses will stem from it's collective resources and group dynamics.

Since success in teams is based upon interdependence among the members, the concept that they have to coordinate their actions has great significance. Within the team each player will have their own role(s); and they must combine their specialized skills to perform at an optimal level. The level of interaction differs from sport to sport and may have an effect on the performance outcome. Each team must capitalize on the resources that are available via the combined talent and abilities of each member. United States Rower Don Smith says, "Man for man we're at least as good as anybody else. It's how we blend together that will make the difference" (McNichol, p. 5).

Group Size

About 100 years ago a French agricultural engineer named Ringelmann did a study with a rope pulling task and found that the average individual performance decreased as the group size increased. Eight-person groups did not pull eight times as hard as their individual efforts but only four times as hard. The people weren't individually recognized or held accountable for their efforts and their evaluation potential decreased as the size of the group increased. Many athletes that feel they "get lost in the crowd" will, at times, not put forth as much effort, not really feeling that it makes a difference. This doesn't hold **as true** in sports where there is high identifiability of members (i.e., pitchers, goalies, kickers). This is why it is so important that every athlete is recognized and held accountable for their specific task. One way to boost individual efforts is to use appropriate incentives to increase motivation, accountability and desired behavior.

In this chapter we have covered what a team is, how a team is formed and many of the characteristics that are necessary for your club to have sound team players and a positive team image. The importance of these things can not be stressed enough. Teamwork and unselfishness create the backbone of a great team, without them, a team can't realistically compete. Taking on this unselfish air may be new to some of you, but in the long run it will help both you and everyone in your organization. This altruistic attitude lends itself to a strongly bonded team, and we will see how important that is next.

Chapter 3
Team Cohesion: How Important is it?

There are many group dynamics that take place within a sporting team. One that has been deemed of immense importance, and the one that will be addressed in this chapter, is that of team cohesion. Cohesion is one of the most powerful group dynamics in the sporting world. You are always hearing about how important it is for a team to gel, bond and have good chemistry. Cohesive teams can achieve some dramatic and awesome things. The way players interact will have a tremendous impact on the way a team performs, as is reflected in this statement by Hall (1960), "The fittest to survive and succeed are those able to find their strength in cooperation, able to build teams based upon mutual helpfulness, and responsibility for one's fellow teammates" (p. 202).

It would seem true then, that cohesion is a means to an end. If cohesion is lacking it can often prevent the team from reaching its' potential. And the more cohesive a team is, the more it lends itself to behaviors that are conducive to peak performance. Shouldn't teams spend time and energy developing a cohesive environment? I think the problem is that many teams aren't sure what cohesion is and how to go about developing and maintaining a cohesive environment. It's more like, if it happens, that's great, and if not, well, we don't have a close group this year and there's not much that can be done. Hopefully, this chapter will help clear up some of these issues.

Defining Cohesion

In the past, the multidimensional concept of cohesion has been defined in many ways. In the sporting world, one definition is most widely used and accepted, and it is the one we will use in this book. Cohesion is the total field of forces which act on members to remain in a particular group (Festinger, Schacter, & Back, 1950). People will usually refer to their team as cohesive if the members get along, are loyal and are united in the pursuit of its goals. Merely being together at workouts and games doesn't necessarily guarantee a team will be cohesive and successful, it simply means that they are occupying the same space at the same time. "You can have a team with 24 superstars and if they are all going in different directions at the same time, there's no cohesiveness, and the team is not going to gel," says Sports Attorney Rockne Lucia, Jr.

A cohesive team can be distinguished from a noncohesive team by many characteristics. A cohesive team has well-defined roles and group norms, common goals, a positive team identity, a good working relationship, shared responsibility, respect, positive energy, trust, a willingness to cooperate, unity, good communication, pride in membership, and synergy. For synergy to take place the action of two or more people must be combined. Syer & Connolly (1984) define synergy as the energy of the perfectly functioning unit and this energy is greater than the sum of the team's individual energies. This supplementary strength may be used to beat a technically superior team. Another indicator of the amount of cohesiveness in a team is the frequency of statements of "we" and "our," in contrast to statements of "I," "me" and "mine." The "we" is just as important as the "me." "Team cohesion is the ability of each team member to accept each individual player as a valuable contributor to the whole," says Joanne Bracker, Women's Basketball Coach, Midland Lutheran College (Brennan, p. 45).

Cohesion can further be divided into two categories, as indicated by Carron's Conceptual System of Cohesion (1982): task cohesion and social cohesion. Task cohesion is the commitment to team goals and performance objectives. Social cohesion encompasses the interpersonal concerns of friendship, affiliation, and emotional support (Gill). He measures these two types in terms of individual attractiveness to a group and group integration. Attractiveness of the group refers to the extent to which the group provides something positive for its members. For example, if a person feels that the group will provide affiliation, friendship, success, etc. for the person, then the group will appear attractive to him. Group integration is how the team functions as one unit. It can be argued that without members' beliefs about the group's potential to fulfill certain personal needs and the existence of group integrity/unity, there is less motivation to maintain the group, and therefore, less group cohesion (Carron, 1985).

The Multidimensional Sports Cohesiveness Questionnaire, developed by Yukelson (1984), measures both task-related and social-related forces. The forces covered can be broken down into four categories. The first is Quality of Teamwork, which measures how well the members work together to achieve successful team performance. The second is Attraction to Group: the member's attraction and satisfaction with the group. The third is Unity of Purpose, which reflects the degree of commitment to the norms, goals, operating procedures, and strategies of the team. The last one is Valued Roles, which assesses the member's sense of identification with the group. It is done from the athlete's perception of the team, which is very important when assessing cohesion.

The purpose for mentioning these two models is to show that cohesion is more than a team "bonding." It is a very complex dynamic that needs to be closely looked at if a team is going to be successful and productive. It is multi-dimensional and encompasses more than the superficial "team members getting along" mentality and effects a team in many ways. Wu Tzu said, "When there is lack of harmony in battle the army cannot win a decisive victory" (Tzu, p. 131).

Facts on Cohesion

There has been a lot of research on the relationship and causality between team cohesion and success. It would seem logical that the more you win the more cohesive the team gets. Although, this is not necessarily always the case. The following studies show some of the different views.

Even though there has been a lot of research on this subject, the relationship between team cohesion and success, up to now, has been equivocal. About twice as many studies say there is a strong relationship between the two than studies that say there is not a strong relationship. Many researchers favor the theory that, due to its dynamic process, cohesion interacts in a circular fashion with other group variables (Carron & Ball, 1977, Hacker & Williams, 1981, Ruder & Gill, 1981).

It is said that cohesion is a dynamic process, that is, everchanging. One thing that is said to have an effect is the level of threat of the competition. It seems to be highest during moderate levels of threat. Teams seemed to be most motivated and cohesive when they were playing a team at their same level or slightly better, as opposed to the #1 or the "worst" team. Which goes right along with the fact that athletes like to be moderately challenged, and feel that they can be successful. If they don't feel that they realistically have a chance they may not be as motivated or bonded in their efforts.

Perception of team cohesion by the players seems to be a key variable. An important factor is if the individuals on the team share a common identity. The team will most likely be more cohesive if they perceive themselves as one unit rather than a bunch of separate entities. Team players want to keep things positive and moving in the right direction. It is also very important that they feel they can exchange ideas and combine their individual resources. Feelings of having a common goal and identity among team members are important. One thing that is very clear is that the team's dynamics are just as important to the success of the team, as are the technical skills and strategies.

Social cohesion is very desirable and can positively affect team performance, if they are committed to their goals. The primary emphasis, though, should be on task cohesion and the adherence to team and individual goals. For example, if players sacrifice what is best for the team to keep friendships strong (social cohesion) this may negatively affect the team's performance. Fielder (1967) points out that on a team where there seems to be extremely close interpersonal ties players may tend to set up shots on the basis on friendship rather than ability, which could be decisive and crucial in competition.

Shared failure may also contribute to cohesion. In a study by Taylor, Doria & Tyler (1983), it was found that when failure occurred on a collegiate men's hockey team, there was a strong tendency to attribute failure to the entire group, rather than to assign blame to one person. A team tends to share responsibility better if they are a cohesive group. They are more willing to decide what action should be taken next, rather than just retreating into their own corners or pointing fingers. Cohesion provides an atmosphere to vent feelings and provides a trusting environment. Conflict can be constructively dealt with due to the fact that the relationships are strong enough to withstand an honest level of challenge and become more resistant to disruptive forces (Corey & Corey).

It has been shown that interacting teams with high cohesion were generally more successful. It seems that success leads to greater cohesion. Evidence seems to support the proposition that causality flows from performance to cohesion. There are still those that feel there is a negative relationship, and yet still, those that feel that it's not a linear process but a circular one. The relationship between factors such as level of cohesion, actual performance and player satisfaction may all work together; although its not known which factor actually starts the trend. Though this does suggest that when a team is more cohesive, they tend to be more successful, and in turn, they have greater satisfaction. Greater satisfaction then leads to higher levels of cohesiveness, and so on.

Regardless of the causality, it can safely be stated that cohesion does play a big role in the dynamics of a team, and is something that teams should not overlook. For our purposes, the research may not be consistent in causality, but one fact remains the same, cohesion is something that won't hinder a team if it is there, and a strong level of cohesion will most likely help it achieve positive results and be successful.

Developing Cohesion

Developing cohesion is something that takes time and effort, but it is well worth the investment. There are some things that need to be present within a team for cohesion to be properly developed:

- ➡ Everyone needs to be on the same page when it comes to team goals. If everyone is striving towards the same thing this will help cohesion develop. Productivity must be established by setting challenging and specific goals. Making sure the members know what the individual goals are, for themselves and their teammates, is very important. If you know what your teammates are striving for, many times you can aid them in their endeavor, which will lead to a more cohesive relationship. Bill Walsh refers to a speech he gave to the Stanford Football team, "You are in an arena that calls for bonding.... From this point forward, we're a group of men who collectively have one common objective, to compete and win" (1990, p. 61). There can be no hidden agendas by any of the members, their goals **must** coincide with team goals. What's good for the team has to be good for the individual and visa versa.
- ➡ Having periodic team meetings is a good way to check in to make sure everything is going alright amongst the team. This provides an opportunity for the team to spend some time together off the field, where it is not so hectic. This way a coach can ask for input, and players can tell others what they see happening, or what they see isn't happening. There is no chaos and no rushing, it is a meeting with the sole purpose of processing what is going on.

Direct assessment, as given by the players, is the most accurate way to determine the amount of cohesiveness on a team. There is not substitute for the player's own perception of what is going on not only for him, but also for the team that he is playing on. How a player views the interworkings on the team is very valuable information when evaluating the level of team cohesion.

1. There should be mutual respect among members. You can't have a cohesive group on the field if you don't respect your teammates. You don't have to necessarily "love" them off the field, but you better "love" them on the field and respect them both on and off the field. You are all fighting for a common goal and there is a special closeness that goes along with this. The 1979 Pittsburgh Pirates demonstrated this with their "We are family" attitude both on and off the field. A sort of "esprit de corps" mentality. Also, when there is a strong level of respect it will also reinforce the merit of a teammate's feedback.
2. There should be effective two-way communication that is clear and direct. Good communication skills result in an increase in self-esteem, respect, trust and decision making skills. Trust is an ongoing process, it will be tested time and time again.
3. There also needs to be a feeling of importance among the team. You should do your best to make each member feel like they are a part of the team and contribute something important. The phrase "treat others as you would like to be treated" applies here. Know the needs of your teammates and how you can help make them feel like they are a viable part of the team. "That's what we call it, a big family, and everyone realizes that and that's why we're so cohesive," San Francisco 49ers Vice President/ Director of the 49ers Foundation, Lisa DeBartolo.
4. Having continuity in practices, and in every part of the team, can contribute to the cohesiveness of the group. Familiarity breeds not only confidence but also a sense of comfort among the team. Also, by placing team members in situations where interaction is necessary, cohesion will increase.

Things to Avoid

There are a few things that, if possible, are best to avoid when trying to establish a cohesive team:

- ➡ Cliques – Cliques become a problem when there is more loyalty to that subgroup than there is to the team as a whole. Unresolved conflict can sometimes be a catalyst to the formation of cliques. Players need to be loyal to all the team members, not just a select few.
- ➡ Excess personnel changes - Excessive personnel changes lead to a decrease in team morale and team performance. The more stability within a particular group, the better off they will be. This allows everyone to develop a good rapport that is secure and cultivated, not something that is being started over again and again with each personnel change.
- ➡ Difficult schedules – It is good to avoid schedules which are too difficult early in the season (if possible). Players may get frustrated and start to blame others (teammates, coaches, parents, etc.).
- ➡ Too much intrateam competition – Some intrateam competition is good, it increases motivation among members, but if there is an excessive amount of it, it can lead to animosity among players and to the cliques we just described above. Intrateam competition should push the players, not divide them.

Variables Influencing Cohesion

1. Stability of membership – The longer members are on a team, the closer they will be, due to the fact that they have reached a certain comfort level with each other. For example, junior college players will have less of a chance to be cohesive because they are usually there for, at the most, two years. There will be

a certain level of cohesion, but since there is a high turnover rate they may not be as cohesive as players at four-year colleges or universities.

2. Role acceptance – If a player doesn't understand or agree with his role on the team, this can have an effect on how much that player feels bonded with other members. If the player has accepted his role he can confidently feel like a strong part of the team.
3. Team size – The smaller a team is, the easier it is to facilitate cohesion. The chances for conflict and feeling left out are decreased since the number of players is reduced.
4. Type of interaction – The relationship between cohesion and performance is often contingent on the level of interdependence between team members. Positive cohesion-performance relationships reported most often are from those team sports requiring extensive interaction and dependence among players, such as basketball, hockey and volleyball. Sports requiring little or no interaction, such as bowling, track or rifle teams, aren't as drastically effected by the level of cohesion.

   For example, baseball and softball are sports that would be considered proactive and reactive dependent. A pitcher would be considered proactive, based on the fact that this one member initiates the action but must depend on others to complete the task. Catchers and position players would be considered reactive dependent because they must wait for the completion of a task by other positions in order to execute their own. For example, the catcher must wait for the pitcher to throw and position players must wait for the ball to be put into play to complete their task. The type of coordination and dependence necessary dictates the extent to which cohesiveness is a factor in successful performance. So in this case, cohesion would be of great importance in determining how successful the team will be.

5. Outcome – If the team won or lost may also have an effect on the way they perceive the level of cohesion on their team. If they did extremely well, they may have that "bask in the glory" syndrome, in which they have yet to come down from the emotional high and may have an overly positive view of things. It is easy to overlook some of the negative things when the season or game ends on a positive note. Or the opposite may occur, in which not only did they play poorly all season, but also ended the season on a bad note; in this case they would probably have a negative view about the level of cohesion in light of the results.

Maintaining Cohesion

Once the team has reached a high level of cohesion, it is important to maintain it at that level. The coach and players need to keep the team on the same track that has gotten them to the point they are at currently. It is imperative that they don't let up on the things that have led to the cohesive atmosphere. Players have to realize that to maintain cohesion they have to give it the same amount of attention they did when they were developing it.

Having periodic team meetings plays an important role in this. It is a time to reflect and ask questions such as "What went well?" "What could use more work?" "What would you like to see more/less of from the coach, yourself, and teammates?". Those are all key questions that will keep everyone on top of things and lets everyone know that they still have to give 110% commitment to keep things going well. Also, you can always improve, there is always you can work on – no matter who you are.

"Even if you're on the right track, you'll get run over if you just sit there." Will Rogers

Having a family atmosphere also helps maintain cohesion. Think about it, in a family there are problems and rough times, but no matter what, family sticks together. There is a strong sense of loyalty, you may have fights, but you will also stand up for those same people if they are being challenged or treated poorly by someone. Being cohesive is especially important during the rough times and could be one of the only things to keep a team motivated when things aren't going well. By having this mentality, athletes will feel it's a given that their teammates will stick by them when it counts. "The thing that has made the 49er organization so special over the years is that I have tried to run the team and organization like we're a family," states San Francisco 49ers Owner Eddie DeBartolo, Jr.

Family attitude builds loyalty and dedication and stems from the perspective that everyone is equal and contributes. The family attitude is something that the great teams have. There is no differentiation between starters and nonstarters, everyone is an important member. Former San Francisco 49er Kicker Jeff Wilkins, feels the same way as the owner of his former team, "When you're part of this team, you're part of a family. You're treated with respect and you also give respect."

Team members don't necessarily have to always get along or be social outside of the sport, but it **will** contribute to your cohesiveness on the field/court. It's not always realistic that 30 people are going to feel like family, but in the heat of competition, you had better have this feeling. One thing that was a common theme among many of the coaches I interviewed was that cohesion was not as necessary for short-term success as it was for a team that was going to be together for a long period of time. For example, cohesion isn't as necessary for an all-star series as it is for each of their respective core teams.

This chapter has taken a look at what cohesion is and how important it is to develop and nurture it on a team – any team. Only good things can come from bonding with other members of your team – good things for everyone, individually and collectively. We have looked at some of the things to avoid: cliques, excessive personnel changes, difficult schedules; which are just as important to know as what should be present: respect, effective communication, feeling of importance, mutual goals, synergy, trust, positive energy, and well-defined roles and norms. All these things are important for a team to function at an optimal level, as stated by Long Beach City College Head Softball Coach Shellie McCall, "Team cohesion is the glue that keeps a team focused and determined to reach its goals."

Chapter 4
What Makes a Great Leader

"Leadership is like gravity. You know it's there, you know it exists, but how do you define it?"
Former San Francisco 49er Tight End, Dr. Jamie Williams

Great leaders come in many forms. In one sense solid leadership is a subjective thing, in another there are certain characteristics that are consensus when it comes to quality leadership. When I think about leadership and the coaches I have had in the past, there is one coach that sticks out in my mind as being an outstanding leader, and incidently, in 1996 he was inducted into the United States Amateur Confederation of Roller Skating's Distinguished Service Hall of Fame – which is certainly no surprise.

Jim Pollard is the kind of leader that, first and foremost, has superior knowledge of competitive artistic roller skating. But, it's not his knowledge of the sport that makes him so special, it's the way he relates to athletes. Even though he was in charge, he still gave you some sense of decision-making responsibility; for example, letting you choose the music you would be skating to, deciding what item would go where in the routine, etc. This gave the athlete an extra sense of accountability when it came to their skating, it certainly did for me. He's so good at what he does and is so well respected, that athletes want to do their best not only for themselves, but also for him. At times, his mere presence was a strong motivating force. He would be the first one to tell you when you did something wrong, and he would also be the first person to tell you when you did something right – neither comment would judge the person, only the behavior. He would criticize technique, never the person. No matter how you were doing technically, he treated you with the same respect and kindness as a person day-in and day-out. After a competition, he always approached it the same whether you bombed or won, first saying what was done well, then telling you what could be improved upon, and always ending on a positive note.

Although this is only my subjective opinion of what makes a great coach, I believe some of the qualities mentioned would hold true for anyone. This chapter will examine what qualities make a good leader and practical ways for people to become better leaders. A "great" leader is hard to define, but they incorporate whatever traits are necessary to motivate others to work hard to pursue their goals. Leadership isn't just a characteristic of one person but rather a complex social relationship. It's the process of influencing members of the group to work hard towards, and be committed to, its' goals. "What makes a good leader is based on your own perceptions. If you move the team and people follow then you are a leader," says former San Francisco 49er, Dr. Jamie Williams.

Leaders can either be task-oriented or person-oriented. Task-oriented leaders are most interested in training, instructing behavior, performance and winning. Person-oriented leaders are more interested in the interpersonal relationships on the team. Great leaders are both task-oriented and people-oriented, but lean more towards being task-oriented and getting things done.

Great leadership requires that you start by taking a look at yourself. Your philosophy of life is usually very close to your philosophy of coaching. It's imperative that you know what your motivation is and what your beliefs and values are. You then need to stick to these core beliefs and values. If you always follow what you believe, then you will have always done the "right" thing. You need to be aware of what your own strengths, weakness and limitations are. Determine in your own heart what qualities make a winner and then direct motivation toward specific ways to develop those characteristics. You must wholeheartedly believe in this philosophy for it will probably be challenged more that once. As a great leader, you need to have a strong personal commitment to the team and yourself. It is also imperative for the team to know what kind of leader they have and what the philosophy of their coach is.

At the beginning of the season you, as the head coach, need to make your philosophy of coaching crystal clear to your athletes. This includes your expectations of the players, of the team as a whole, and let them know what kind of coach you are. You must be consistent, follow through and be consciously aware of team progress, as well as team problems, and how they fit in with the philosophy and standards you have set. A rapport needs to be developed between you and the players, you and your assistants, and among the players themselves. At this time, the rules should be made clear and players should ask questions regarding the rules so there is no confusion later on down the road. The rules must be consistent and hold true for everyone, no exceptions. Inconsistency in the implementation of the rules can lead to team dissention. Team rules give clarity, it becomes a black and white issue – if you go outside the rules there will be consequences. The coach has to be firm in regards to rules.

You need to be an inspiring leader and set the pace for the team members. The team learns from you and will model your behavior. Teach players to respect one another equally by your example. Everything starts from the top down. In professional sports, it starts with the owner and then trickles down. In college and on Olympic teams, it starts with the head coach. The players learn from you how to gather information, set goals, consider alternatives, get support and meet deadlines. You are in a position to give new challenges and expose your players to new competition and experiences. If you respect, understand and listen to your athletes, you won't lose power or control – you'll gain it (Huang & Lynch).

Keep in mind, the things you want to teach to your athletes you must first possess yourself. For example, if you want them to be confident, have a strong belief in what they are doing, have self-control, be disciplined, etc., then you must first possess all these traits yourself. San Francisco 49ers Owner Eddie DeBartolo, Jr. says that the best kind of leadership is to lead by example, "this way you're not asking anybody to do anything you can't or haven't done (or tried to do)." You have a hard job, you have to remain a strong leader, while at the same time, be viewed as approachable by your players. You serve as an influential role model for your players and everything you do will be watched, and many times scrutinized. Vince Lombardi says, "Leaders are made, they are not born; and they are made just like anything else has every been made in this country – by hard work" (Dowling, 1970, p. 179).

Former San Francisco 49er, Dr. Jamie Williams talks about Joe Montana, Ronnie Lott, Roger Craig and Jerry Rice leading by example, "People will follow if they see you get down and dirty, when they see you sell out they will follow." Leading by example is a very powerful tool, your words and your actions are in sync, and this is very important. San Francisco 49er Marquez Pope speaks on leadership, "Some people are vocal, some nonvocal. The main thing is demonstrating your work ethic. You do it over and over and it shows results. You lead by the results you produce."

Great leaders are scholars in their field and are intelligent. Like all great scholars, they aren't know-it-alls, they feel there is always more to learn and they have a willingness to admit mistakes. As a coach, you shouldn't make assumptions, you should make decisions based on facts. "By staying present and aware of what is happening the leader can do less and achieve more" (Tzu, p. 93). Great leaders apply common sense and simplicity to complex tasks. You must select the right strategy for the right situation, even when the pressure is overwhelming. They are well organized, detail-oriented and are rarely caught off guard due to their thorough preparation.

Their great knowledge, in turn, allows them to be great educators and motivators. They are also smart enough to know that many times they will have to alter what they originally planned due to changing circumstances – so flexibility and having an open mind are very important.

"A successful leader plans his work, and work his plan."
Napoleon Hill

The great leaders are not only highly driven and intrinsically motivated, but they also foster the same sort of enthusiasm in their players. Charles Schwab says, "I consider my ability to arouse enthusiasm among the men the greatest asset I possess, and the way to develop the best that is in a man is by appreciation and encouragement" (Carnegie, 1964, p. 34). They have a high energy level, project that energy, create task excitement, and are catalysts for positive action. You need to be a good motivator and have the gift for verbal persuasion. You have to get your athletes to "buy in" to the fact that hard work does pay off and that the pursuit of excellence is a tough journey, but a worthwhile one. You can't take motivation for granted. Even the players that are always motivated can use some outside motivation from coaches. You have to always be encouraging them, as people and as players.

It is up to the coach to provide an environment where the athletes can practice the strategies that will help them perform at an optimal level on a consistent basis. You need an environment where athletes will feel comfortable and will enjoy spending their time. You want to reduce the uncertainties to the best of your ability. There are so many variables that are out of your control that it's in the team's best interest to take care of the things that are within your control as best as possible.

Greatness in leadership encompasses confidence and assertiveness. You have enough confidence in your abilities, the abilities of the members, and in the level of preparedness to keep your pose in tough situations. You take calculated risks, are innovative and confident in your decision to do so; realizing that being timid will not get you where you want to go. This confidence and assertiveness will usually, again, like everything else, trickle down to the team members. The quality and effectiveness of a great leader will often show itself by way of the team's effort as a whole. By having a lot of confidence in your team, many times this will give them added strength to do extraordinary things.

You must have respect for your players and work as hard as the team. We spoke about respect in the preceding chapter, but it is worth mentioning again here. If you treat your athletes with genuine respect, they will respect you and, most likely, go to any lengths for you and the team. I say genuine because players can usually tell if it is phony and won't take it to heart. Coaches need to treat everyone with **equal** respect and honesty, and the players will in turn do the same. Don't play favorites, it puts too much pressure on the athlete, may alienate him from his teammates, and lower the self-esteem of the others. Be consistent and always follow through with what you say, this way you will always maintain your credibility with the players. Former San Francisco 49er, Dr. Jamie Williams says, "Leadership is based on results. Great leadership is based on results and credibility."

Simply put, treat them right and they will treat you right. Sincerity in coaching can not be stressed enough. If you meet the needs of your athletes, you will, at the same time, be meeting your own needs. "Be generous with small tokens of appreciation they will multiply in returned loyalty and service" (Roberts, 1987, p. 79). You often hear players talk about how they want to give something back to the coach/owner who has shown respect for them and given them the opportunity to play. "...'I'm going to care about you, and if your wife gets sick I'm going to send her flowers.' You have to have a reason for doing that – it has to come from the heart. I think I've gotten back on the field," says San Francisco 49ers Owner Eddie DeBartolo,

Jr. Treat people with respect and they'll be united and will want to do well for you, for themselves and the team.

To get the most out of each player and make the team experience a positive one, you must understand the individuality of your players and the dynamics of group interaction. Knowing the patterns in the evolvement of a group will give you a valuable perspective. It's essential to know the needs, strengths and weaknesses of your athletes. Great leaders must see into the hearts and heads of their players. They must know what makes each of them tick and how they are motivated. It's hard to be responsive to their needs if you are unsure of what they are! That's why it is imperative to know the mental make-up of your athletes. The team's character changes as the athletes change and you have to know the type of team you are dealing with; for example, is it a tough team, strong team, rough-playing team, confident team, etc.

It is your job to know your players well enough to be able to take their strengths and weaknesses and use them to their fullest potential within the context of the team. Systematic delegation, which is getting the right players doing the right job, is vital on teams; for example, choosing the best person for team captain, it has to be someone who you feel has the right qualities. It can be to the team's disadvantage if you don't know where your players will best be utilized. This is why it is so important for you to get to know each of your players as well as possible.

From there, you then have to find ways to challenge your athletes. Challenge, not threaten, one is positive and raises self-esteem, the other is negative and can have the opposite effect. Nothing good comes out of negativity, no matter which way you look at it. You need to appeal to the spirit of the team. You must be intuitive enough to know when to challenge and when to step back. This all stems from knowing your athletes well, having a knack for reading people, and tuning into your players without judgment or labeling. Players will express their feelings or problems persistently until they are dealt with. Coaches need to be aware of this. If they are, then they are better able to see problems before they arise and take the appropriate action. In essence, you must have good instincts and be a quick reactor.

The great leader is a master in the art of communication. He is aware of the strong need for his actions to match his words. Leaders need to possess a willingness to listen to input with an open mind. Two-way communication is essential in a team environment. Being approachable and having an "open door" policy makes for very good relations among the team. This is crucial in building a trusting and open environment. It must be an established norm that it is okay to ask for help. It's critical that the players feel that they can communicate openly without fear of punishment.

There has to be a "feedback loop" where the players give input and tell you what they think, and you have to give players both constructive criticism and positive feedback – it's a circular process. Firmness and fairness are important components in this. The way you communicate with and lead your team will play a big part in your player's motivation to play hard. Disclose things that you feel will strengthen your relationship with them, as well as the relationship they have with their teammates. You should not use your role to protect yourself from honest and direct interaction with the players. Feedback from the players, and to the players, is a very meaningful thing in sports.

You must let it be known that you are there for the players, in any capacity, but as a coach, not a friend, and that you will be supportive of them. It is essential that coaches make themselves available to the players, whether it is to discuss sports, personal problems, grades, etc. John Madden says, "Too many coaches want to be 'one of the guys', but that's the worst thing a coach can be ... Your players need a coach, a teacher, not a friend" (Conner, 1988, p. 107). Exceptional leaders have the ability to be empathetic, and are able to see things from the perspective of their players. They are there to help the players along, not to exploit them on their own behalf or to enhance their own ego. This means that the player knows the coach will do what he can and will act in the best interest of the athlete, as well as the team as a whole. It is the coach's responsibility to balance what is best for the individual with what is best for the whole team.

The goal is to push the team to perform to their full potential. You, along with the players, have to set obtainable yet demanding team goals. Strong leadership becomes a moot point if the players are uninterested in the mission and goals. You must develop a strong rapport, and you all need to be on the same page – this involves trust and confidence on both ends. "Good leadership consists of motivating people to their highest levels by offering them opportunities, not obligations" (Tzu, p. 135). They provide opportunities to fulfill their goals and dreams. Outstanding leaders are able to influence others to work toward their goals.

Murray & Mann stated that a proficient leader "has a vision, an intense focus on outcome and results, a realistic strategy to carry out the vision and the ability to communicate the vision and rally support of others" (Williams, 1993, p. 87). Leaders are there to coach, direct and nudge players in the direction of the goals. They have a strong ability to pass their intensity along to their others. They are always "in" the game right along with the players. Former San Francisco 49er, Dr. Jamie Williams says, "You can be a leader that leads people down the wrong path, into chaos. When a coach takes over a team he's a leader, when a quarterback takes the field, he's a leader. That doesn't mean he's going to take them where they need to go. But he will take them somewhere. The ones with great integrity and credibility will take them where they need to go and will have great followship."

A leader guides a team, not rules a team. He charts a course, gives direction and develops the social and psychological environment (Martens, 1987). Ultimately, you are responsible for providing a great atmosphere for players to learn, grow and help them identify obstacles in the path you are providing for them. You must give some responsibility to the group and have the courage to foster independence. Otherwise the members will feel that you don't trust them to take care of themselves, and will thus live up to this expectation by being irresponsible. There must be a balance where you accept your rightful share of responsibility and give some back to the team members.

Great leaders have physical and mental stamina – they are able to withstand pressure and are aware of their own energy level. This is very important to help prevent burnout in coaching. The most effective coaches are the ones who can use the least effort and get the desired results. Having a sense of humor will help you keep things in perspective and so they don't seem overwhelming. Maintain this perspective and never lose sight of the big picture. You need to stay on an even keel – moodiness is not a quality of a great leader. Moody coaches create an atmosphere of worry, tension and fear.

Staff Cohesion

It is important for the coaches to adhere to all the principles of team building. In a sense, they are their own mini-team. Take time when selecting assistant coaches because they will determine the collective potential the team has. These are very important decisions and should be thought out. If there is dissention in the coaching staff it effects the team as a whole. There must be synergy among the coaching staff and the same principles of a common goal and vision must be evident. The chemistry within the staff is critical to its' productiveness. Every coach has their own unique personality. It is best to have coaches with complementary personalities that are able to work well together, as well as with the players.

Assistant coaches need to be active, not passive. They each have their own area of expertise and their own strengths and weaknesses. They operate as their own team. They are there because of their abilities, and it is up to you, as the head coach, to listen to the input and feedback from assistants to best serve the team. Division of leaders will be sensed by players, they will feel confused by it and it could have a detrimental effect on the team.

You must allow your assistants to be creative and speak up freely with ideas and input. You hired these people for a reason, so you need to have full trust in them. If you delegate an assignment don't go back and try to do it yourself, show faith in the person/people you delegated to. You need to share and capitalize on each other's strengths and build on each other's ideas. Take a genuine interest in what they have to say. Also, be receptive to the needs of your assistants. Think back to when you were an assistant coach and the things you liked and didn't like in relation to the head coach.

Conflict between coaches usually arise for one of two reasons: 1) they are too much alike; or 2) competition. Many times if they are too much alike; for example, stubborn, it can cause them to butt heads on some issues – neither person wanting to let up. Secondly, there can sometimes be competition between coaches, many times control issues are at the heart of this. Assistants need to keep in mind the characteristics they would want in assistants if they were a head coach and act accordingly. Never forget that you are all on the same side, and want the same things for the team.

This chapter has looked at a number of characteristics that seem to go hand in hand with outstanding leadership. Excellence in leadership is acquired by people who have a strong sense of vision, have passion and are able to get people to commit 100% and take the necessary action to see that vision become a reality. The skills that great leaders excel in are: the art of communication and motivation, mutual respect, instilling confidence and enthusiasm, and showing credibility and integrity on a stable basis.

Chapter 5
Communication is the Key

The art of communication is something that tends to be overlooked, and/or taken for granted, in teams - until there is a breakdown in that communication. Then it becomes a hot topic. Teams shouldn't wait until there is a breakdown to address and improve on its communication skills. This chapter will look at ways to improve communication and listening skills among teams, since communication is a key ingredient in a team working well together and being successful.

We tend to communicate with others in two ways: with words and with body language. You must be consistent in both verbal and behavioral communication. It is said that body language, gestures and facial expressions account for as much as 50-75% of communication (Weinberg, 1988). You constantly need to watch, and be aware of, your body language (gestures, facial expressions, voice inflections, posture changes). Many times, how you say something is more significant than what you are actually saying. You must follow what is said with the appropriate actions and be consistent with content and emotion. People tend to remember 75% of what they hear and see - so if your actions and words are in sync it will be the most powerful. The foundation for communication is mutual respect and trust for all members of the team. Remember, it's not just what you say, but how you say it. It is important for there to be effective 2-way communication between players and coaches and among the players themselves. As a coach, you must have credibility among your team for your players to **really hear** what you are communicating to them.

Game Day Communication

You shouldn't change anything in the way you communicate with your team just because it is game day. Your game approach should be the same as your practice approach. You must stay consistent and never show any signs of panic in either your body language or your voice. You should communicate in an even tone going over the basics of what needs to be done and, if you deem it appropriate, you can remind them of what they've sacrificed to be here (6:00 am practices, long days, etc.). Use time-outs to build confidence by being positive, adjust the game plan if necessary, and stress the goals that have been set.

There also needs to be clear communication among the players on the field/court. If there is lack of communication on the field it can cost you a run, or contribute to a victory for the other team. Confusion on your part can be detrimental to the team. Signs, verbals and cues must be well known so that there isn't any disarray or chaos in the heat of competition. For example, if a catcher is unsure of signs and has to keep starting over, it can disrupt the rhythm of the pitcher.

After a good performance (I don't say after a win, because a team can play great and still lose the game) it is important to give a lot of positive feedback as to what went well and contributed to the exceptional quality performance. It is also just as important to go over the areas where improvements can still be made. After a poor performance (again, you can still win even if the performance wasn't up to par) it is important to find things that were positive, then point out what wasn't executed properly and needs to be worked on, and finish up with something encouraging to keep them motivated and positive for the next game and/or practice. Also, never reprimand an individual in front of the team, only praise them. Reprimanding them in public can be damaging to their self-esteem. If a player did something that was costly during the game, he knows it, the coach shouldn't make it worse by yelling at him in front of the whole team.

Basically, you should approach both in a similar fashion. Whether it was a win or loss, the approach should be the same. You should praise what they did well, give your critique, and then finish up with something positive and encouraging. Former coach for New Orleans Saints, Bum Phillips, said, "People are human. If you are going to criticize them, compliment them first" (Chieger & Sullivan, 1990, p. 27).

Ways to improve communication

1. Communicate with each other as individuals - Don's call them by their number (#32) or position (starting shortstop), but by their name. Ask questions about other things besides sports, show an interest in how they are doing, as a person, not just as a player. Say positive things to athletes unrelated to sports as well.
2. Have players give written feedback on coaches in addition to fellow teammates. This can give some helpful and good information to spur topics at team meetings. This way the coach isn't doing all the talking, the players are saying something as well. Candidly share your point of view and encourage teammates and coaches to do the same. The better the communication, the closer your team will be, and, as a result, the better you will play.
3. You also might want to have players select captains that can best represent their interests and then have weekly meetings with those captains. This will improve the player-coach relationship by gaining the necessary information to keep the team flowing in a positive manner. As a coach, you need to be able to see things from someone else's point of view. Maybe ask your players, "What would you do if you were coach for a week?" Have your captain get written feedback from the players that they can pass on to you - this may give you some added insight into your players.
4. It's important to have periodic team meetings as well, which provide the forum for players to give feedback to their teammates as well as get input from coaches. Keep in mind that, if you do have something critical to say, do it in the best way possible - so the person hears you and doesn't feel like they are being put on

the defensive. It's best to follow this simple rule – the "sandwich technique." Start out by saying something positive to the person ("I've noticed you've been working really hard – that's great."); then move on to your constructive criticism ("One thing that might be helpful is if you ...."); and, then finish up with another positive statement ("Keep up the good work – I have a lot of confidence in you."). With this technique, the players will be more receptive to what you have to say. *ALWAYS END ON A POSITIVE NOTE!*

Exercise #3

Sit in a circle and say one thing you appreciate about the person sitting next to you. This will open up communication and improve team relations. Do this periodically (i.e., every third team meeting to help keep the environment positive) to keep the lines of communication open and the team morale high.

5. Be a good listener:

- ✔ Paraphrase for verification/acknowledgment (nod head), this way you can question as well as clarify what you are hearing. "What I hear you saying is that ... " This will help avoid any misunderstandings and let the other person know that you are actively listening. You have to really concentrate to get the full scope of what the other person is saying.
- ✔ Invite the person to open up and say more (expand on thoughts), be encouraging and show empathy.
- ✔ Summarize what is being relayed.
- ✔ Positively reinforce the fact that the person is expressing their feelings and thoughts to you. This will encourage this behavior to be a regular occurrence.

6. Having an open door policy is crucial – Letting the players know that they can come and talk to the coach about whatever is on their mind (basketball, school, social problems, etc.) is very important. Having this open communication will establish a norm that will be conducive to optimal performance. They must be encouraged to openly express ideas and opinions. Questions should be welcomed.
7. Potential problems that may get in the way of you being a good listener are: preparing what you are going to say while the other person is still talking; interrupting to give your opinion, rather than waiting for the person to finish their thought; and listening out of obligation rather than with a desire to really understand what that person is saying and where they are coming from.

Problem solving

Clear communication will also lend itself to sound problem-solving skills. If you avoid conflict it can lead to more serious problems. Confrontations are a part of sports – if a team is to improve, it will face challenges and adversity. Conflict tends to grow out of mistrust and unresolved issues. Effective problem solving has to start from a foundation of mutual trust as well as a common desire to improve. You need to:

- ✔ Recognize and agree on the problem(s) – One person may think the problem is one thing, while the other may think it is something totally different. Think about what you are going to say before you say it, don't let your emotions do all the talking.
- ✔ Describe the situation – Talk about any patterns surrounding this problem and go over it in detail. You also need to determine what seems to be the cause of

the problem. Many times, problems between coaches and players have to do with the interpretation of a behavior, rather than the behavior itself. They both interpret it differently and until they communicate the differences there will continue to be problems. If you are wrong, admit it sincerely. Let the person know you have a strong desire to understand their position.

✔ Brainstorm ideas – Together discuss different ways that you feel this can be dealt with and collectively come up with strategies to try and resolve it. Be specific, concise and just talk about the facts.

✔ Come to an agreeable resolution – Take the necessary steps to try and deal with this and together evaluate progress intermittently. (Fisher, Rayner & Belgard, 1995).

Feedback

The need for regular performance feedback must be established. Having continuous feedback will help the proper behavior/actions become a habit. Sharing feedback is something players may shy away from at first because it may seemingly leave them vulnerable. Keep this in mind when players come to you. Feedback directs behavior and increases motivation. Give explanations for the corrections, and then listen to what the athlete is expressing to you regarding the feedback.

Feedback that lacks credibility may jeopardize the relationship between the player and coach. The benefits of feedback depend on how receptive the player is, the approach the coach takes and the validity of the information that is being conveyed. Team, as well as individual feedback, is very important to a group's success. Without this, the team will not be able to change and grow.

There must be a willingness to both give and receive feedback. It must be timed well and given in a constructive way. The athletes must feel they are in an environment where they are given the opportunity to use their full range of abilities and reach their potential. The norm for this should be established early in the development of the group. Positive feedback almost always has a greater impact than negative feedback does. Feedback that describes specific behavior is rated as more effective than interpretive or mixed feedback. Constructive criticism is taken better and given more credibility if given after positive feedback and is then followed by more positive feedback (the sandwich technique). You don't want to give feedback on too many different areas at one time, it can be overwhelming.

When giving feedback, describe your observations of the specific behavior, don't critique the person's attitude or personality. It is important that you express your feelings, not judgements. Sharp negative criticisms and judgements tend to put players on the defensive and arouse resentment. Communicate things that are helpful not harmful – ask yourself, "Is what I'm saying significant to the team (or player)?"

Feedback is best when given during the act (concurrent feedback) or right after the completion (terminal feedback) of a task. It is recommended that you use the ratio of 2:1 when giving feedback and constructive criticism – this goes hand-in-hand with the sandwich technique mentioned earlier. Communicate the process, not just the solution – communicate what you want done, not what you want avoided. Many times the thing you want avoided most of all comes to fruition due to the coach constantly telling the player "not" to do that.

The feedback needs to be timely, informative and brief. There is no need for excessive verbiage. Deal in specifics and stay focused on the issue, don't bring up the past unless it has direct relevance. It is also important that you make only justified statements. That is, provide backup for what you are saying. Showing statistics can be a good way of doing this. They provide a neutral basis for a discussion on ways to improve. You always need to be ready to explain unclear messages and answer questions.

It's is also important to respond to both correct and incorrect execution. If you speak to them only when mistakes are made it can effect their self-confidence and they will shy away from you. Also, praise the slightest improvement in a skill that a player is learning or having trouble with. This will provide an atmosphere where the athletes will welcome feedback and respond positively to it.

When receiving feedback it's vital that you don't interrupt and don't react immediately. Keep an open mind, seek further clarification, and keep things in perspective. Try to get all the information first, when we lack some of the information we tend to fill in the blanks with pessimistic information that we have created. Remember, you have 2 ears and one mouth, use them accordingly.

For communication to be effective you not only have to listen and absorb what is being said, but you also have to retain the information and/or feedback. You need to store it in your memory bank, not let it go in one ear and out the other. You may need to refer back to what you were told at an later date when theinformation may be more applicable.

Success in all facets of your life will be influenced by your ability to be an effective communicator. There must be a good rapport for there to be successful communication, this means you must feel comfortable going to your coaches, teammates, family member, boss or coworkers when there is something on your mind. And, everyone must constantly be aware of what it means to be a good communicator – being able to say the right thing, at the right time, in the right way. This encompasses being a good listener, proficient problem solver, and good at giving and receiving feedback – all of the things that were talked about in this chapter and are crucial to a team running smoothly.

Chapter 6
Getting Motivated

Everyone always talks about "being motivated," "getting motivated" and "staying motivated." But what is motivation? And why is it so important in sports? Just as learning to play catch is the first step in many sports, motivation is the first step to having a solid mental approach to sports. You have to possess the motivation to take the necessary steps to reach a pinnacle in your performance.

What is Motivation?

Motivation is the psychological force that pushes and drives you to work hard – it's the reason that operates as a catalyst to action. Motivation is a state of heart and mind. It's continually seeking out and meeting new challenges, identifying what you love to do and filling your life with that. It's this passion, inner drive and desire that keeps you going each and every day.

For coaches, motivation is finding a way to, number one, keep themselves going; and number two, get players to do things they might not always want to do on their own but is in their best interest. For players, it's the reason that they act, or fail to act. In most sports, the season is long; it is one of endurance – physical and mental endurance. The team that endures over the long haul is the one that will most likely come out on top. Staying inspired and driven for the whole season is a definite challenge, it takes a lot of energy to uphold a high level of motivation. It is crucial for players to stay motivated both mentally **and** physically.

Your attitude plays a big role in how motivated and persistent you will be in your endeavors. Attitudes are based on your beliefs and are reinforced by your emotions about a certain topic or situation. These attitudes predispose you to behave in certain ways. You cognitively process information, then you have either a positive or negative belief about it that results in a certain behavior reinforced by your emotions. Sometimes your attitude about yourself is so familiar that you don't recognize the fact that it is counterproductive to what you're trying to achieve. Attitudes and expectations are strong determinants of how persistent you will be and how successful you will become because they effect the way you feel mentally and physically.

Motivation has 2 components: 1) intensity of behavior – arousal; and 2) direction of behavior (Gill):

1. Arousal can be defined as a general state of activation or excitement that ranges from deep sleep to extreme excitement. When there is increased arousal the body reacts to this stress with the "fight or flight" response of the autonomic nervous system. Individuals manifest anxiety in different ways, and the level of arousal has a direct effect on performance.

   Take, for example, the Olympics – the pressure and excitement can bring extraordinary performances and record breaking bests or you can choke. I remember when I was competing as a skater, every year at the Regional Competition a lot of athletes would skate above themselves – meaning that they would do things during the practice sessions and competition that they weren't able to do during the year. The adrenaline of being at such a big meet pushed the skaters past what they thought their limits were. This is not uncommon, many athletes tend to perform above themselves at the big competitions. Or, athletes will go the other way and completely choke. The difference at big games is the emotional management, that is what separates the good athletes from the great athletes. Psychologist Cristina Versari says, "All Olympic athletes are excellent at their sport and on any given day any one of them could win. The only real difference between them is their ability to control their emotion" (Murray, 1996, p. 6).

The Drive Theory states that increased arousal increases the likelihood of your dominant response to occur. If the skill is simple or well learned increased arousal will improve performance. If arousal is high, you will tend to go to what is most comfortable and is habitual for you, so hopefully what is comfortable is what you should be doing! The Inverted-U Theory, which is the most favored, states that an moderate level of arousal is required for the best performance. So, you need to find out what your optimal arousal level is. A higher level of arousal is necessary for optimal performance in gross motor activities (strength, endurance and speed). But, a high level interferes with performing complex skills (fine muscle movement, coordination, steadiness and general concentration).

The presence of others seems to increase arousal and leads to the performance of their dominant response; and if this dominant response is correct, performance will be that much better. Both Dan O'Brien and Carl Lewis made mention of the positive effect of the home crowd at the 1996

Summer Olympics in Atlanta. It was also commented on a number of times how the fan support during the gymnastics was so overwhelming. Many times with such increased arousal, you find your "hidden reserve." You are past your normal breaking point, but because of the excitement you are still able to go on. It was not only helpful to the Americans, but it also distracted many of the competitors from other countries. The Americans were quite comfortable in their home environment and they responded to the increased arousal with their dominant response (which was based on being well trained and prepared) and yielded positive results.

Exercise #4

Go over your best performance and figure out what your arousal level was, give yourself a rating from 1(barely aroused) to 5 (extremely aroused). Also, start keeping track of your arousal level during practices and games, noting if your performance was, or was not, where you want it to be in relation to your arousal level. This will help you determine what your optimal arousal level is. Research shows that a slightly above average level is preferable to a normal or subnormal arousal state.

2. The second component is direction of behavior. You need to find out if you are motivated to move towards something (reward) or move away from something (punishment). Consensus is that the things that get rewarded get done and anything not reinforced will dissipate.

✔ Positive reinforcement – When you do something correct you get something. For example, when you do something right you get to pick the drills for the day. Positive reinforcement strengthens behavior.

- ✔ Negative reinforcement – When you do something correct, something negative is eliminated. For example, you don't have to do any running after practice. Negative reinforcement also strengthens behavior.
- ✔ Punishment – Something negative is presented to the athlete, or something positive is taken away. An example of punishment would be to make the athlete do extra running or take him out of the line-up for a game. Generally speaking, punishment will weaken the behavior. But be careful, sometimes punishment can reinforce undesirable behavior by drawing attention to it. So, sometimes it's best to ignore it, unless it is disruptive to the entire team.

Punishment can eat away at motivation and leave people with bad feelings and hostility. One way many coaches punish athletes is to suspend them from one or more games. This tends to work because competition is a place for the athlete to showcase his talents and test his limits. Most athletes do not like to be deprived of this since we all have an innate tendency and desire to compete. Many times the threat of punishment can force athletes to work harder, but this doesn't always mean that their skills will improve. Keep in mind though, too much or too little discipline makes any sort of discipline less effective – there needs to be a balance. You have to enforce the rules and standards that have been set by the coach at the beginning of the season. (See the progression, it all goes back to what is done when the team is being formed!)

Types of motivation

There are two types of motivation - intrinsic and extrinsic. Intrinsic motivation is when you participate in sports for the fun and satisfaction you derive from it. You do it for the pride you feel and all the internal intangibles unique to you. It is the "innate, natural propensity to engage one's interests and exercise one's capacities, and in doing so, to seek and conquer optimal challenges" (Deci & Ryan, 1985, p. 43). You may get an external reward, but that is not the main reason that you were motivated. Extrinsic motivation is when you do it solely for external reasons such as money, awards, trophies, prestige, all the outside things. You become consumed with a "what am I going to get for doing this" mentality.

There must be a combination of intrinsic and extrinsic motivation, and it can shift back and forth. There may be times when your intrinsic motivation is stronger and times when your extrinsic motivation is stronger. You especially have to be aware of what your motivation is when you are a professional athlete. It becomes harder to keep your intrinsic motivation when you are being rewarded so heavily externally. The consequences of winning take on a whole new meaning – many times your job is on the line. It can be easy to lose sight of some of the reasons you started in your sport in the first place if you are not careful. You must retain your joy for the sport and not let the needs of others intrude. The problem with extrinsic rewards is that after time they too can lose their motivational power.

Here's an example: There's this young girl who is a competitive skater, and while she was learning a new jump her parents gave her a dollar every time she landed it. She practiced and practiced, and after she mastered the jump, her parents no longer gave her a dollar. Then, when the money stopped she didn't want to practice it because she wasn't being rewarded externally anymore. This is a perfect illustration of how external rewards can undermine intrinsic motivation and be viewed as having a controlling effect. The absence of external rewards is often the measure of intrinsic motivation.

How you interpret the reward is the important factor, not necessarily the reward itself. So, if you don't think that the reward is controlling and feel you can maintain your intrinsic motivation, then your motivation is not diminished. Having a peak performance just once, many times provides the constant intrinsic motivation necessary to keep pushing and pushing to feel it again and again. This is what drives the best athletes, wanting to experience that feeling of doing their best over and over. They are self-motivators, driven by something internal.

"The great athletes are not motivated by money, the ones that are true, true competitors. I don't think you can get players like Montana, Craig, Lott, Rice, Young and other players we have, motivated strictly by money. Their sense of pride, sense of duty, sense of their jobs, and future is very important. They are self-motivators," says San Francisco 49ers Owner Eddie DeBartolo, Jr. Intrinsic motivation seems to be the key. The intangible rewards of athletics should be more important than the monetary gains. It's all about striving to do your personal best.

Team Motivation

The desire for group success is a group-oriented motive, the basis of which is the member's disposition to derive pride and satisfaction with the team if it is successful in accomplishing the task (Zander, 1971). Success being defined as the achievement of something desired, intended or attempted. There must be an individual commitment to a group effort. Sports teams in themselves are natural incentives in the way of friendship, affiliation, and social support and provide the forum for cohesion to be developed. "A team offers a path of self-discovery in a community context" (Syer & Connolly, p. 117). Also, seeing your teammates do well can serve as motivation. A player can often build on the momentum of the team. There are social pressures in athletics, as in all other aspects of life, a need to be liked and excepted by our peers. "We're all social animals with the need to be liked and respected, to both fit in with others and yet to standout sufficiently so that our individual worth is recognized" (Tutko & Tosi, 1976, p. 27). We are motivated by a need to feel worthy and valued in all of our ventures.

The group needs to be motivated, but in a way so as not to destroy the intrinsic motivation of the individual. Each player may be driven by different things, one for the social affiliation and another might be there to win and hopefully get drafted. The team as a whole must have the common desire to be successful, be willing to risk losing, and possess that competitive drive. Among themselves they must maximize their efforts and develop pride and confidence in their team. Recognition by teammates and coaches is a strong motivator and helps sustain cohesion on a team. Enthusiasm is also a strong motivator and is very contagious. The more enthusiasm you show, the more your teammates will likely display. This will push every player in pursuit of their goals. Group motivation will stay high if its goals are clearly defined and there is a fair amount of probability of reaching those goals.

There must be pride in yourself and your team. Pride is a strong motivational factor in sports as well as every aspect of your life. You must feel pride in what you've accomplished as an individual, and pride in the organization you are a part of. Lisa DeBartolo comments on what makes the 49ers organization so successful and what motivates them, "Pride – everyone who works in the organization, from upper management to the security guards, are proud of it. That feeling radiates throughout the whole business." You must be so full of pride that you are going to stay committed and persevere no matter what. This pride will fuel your commitment to the goals you have set for yourself. Possess the desire to stay committed so that you look good to yourself, not to others.

The motivation is evident in great teams, during both good and bad times. These teams know what they want, have a plan to get there, and are relentless in their efforts to get it. The game must have a redeeming value to everyone on the team. The deciding factor between the team that wins and the one that loses is the mental attitude, mental toughness and mental dedication of the team as a whole.

Why is motivation lost?

There are many reasons why an athlete might suffer from low motivation, or lose it completely, and here we will address some of the more common ones:

1. No fun – Motivation is directly proportional to the pleasure received from participating. If there is no fun derived from it, motivation will be negatively effected. If there is no team spirit this can be one reason why the sport has lost its enjoyment.
2. Fear of failure – In this instance, the motivation is to avoid a threat to self-worth. So, motivation isn't necessarily lost, it's just going in the opposite direction. This creates an outward focus, rather than an inward focus. You then become tentative and don't work as hard, this way you have an excuse to fall back on (e.g., going out and partying the night before a game). In this case, performance is poor, and ability is not questioned, just attributed to, say, lack of sleep. If performance is good than this just augments your ability in everyone's eyes. This is called a self-serving bias – if it's a good outcome you will attribute it to your effort and abilities; and if the outcome is bad you will say it had to do with something external and beyond your control. This can create tension and doubt about abilities. Ego involvement can play a big part in not attributing failure to personal shortcomings. Many times you will act like you just don't care one way or another to protect yourself from getting hurt. You feel this nonchalant attitude will be a good cover up. In reality, the only person you are trying to fool with this is yourself. You will do anything to protect your ego, and this means blaming anyone and anything for you not playing well.

Excuses shield the athlete from failure and loss of self-esteem – it's a protection mechanism. Players that are afraid of failure tend to play conservatively/ tentatively in hopes that their opponent will be the one to make the mistake and "give it away." They are afraid of letting others down. And, as a result, aren't always as aggressive as they should be. As a coach, you need to encourage players to learn from failure and separate their identity and self-worth from their performance.

3. Unmet needs – Athletes participate in sports to have their needs met; needs such as fun, learn/improve skills, affiliation/socialize, exchange ideas, succeed/ demonstrate competency. These needs are shown by Maslow's (1968) needs hierarchy. The most basic needs are those for food, water and safety. The need for friendship and a sense of belonging to a social group are deficiency needs. Then there are esteem needs – when individuals draw respect from others and are able to gain pride from their efforts. The last one is self-actualization – herein lies the need to put forth the necessary effort to maximize use of whatever innate talents you possess and develop a sense of who you are and your place in the grand scheme of things (Russell). If the needs that you are trying to meet by participating in sports aren't being met, then your motivation will be diminished.
4. Excessive pressure to perform – If the perceived pressure is just too overwhelming and you feel unable to cope, you might just stops trying. You just sort of shut down and may end up leaving your sport (often prematurely).
5. Learned helplessness – You feel that no matter what you do it's either not good enough or won't make a difference so you just say, "Oh well, I can't do it so

why bother trying" and give up. You feel you have no real control and failure is inevitable, and this is why motivation is lost. You attribute failure to stable, uncontrollable factors. Right along with this is outcome expectancy. If a player estimates that a given behavior will lead to certain outcomes then he is more apt to move forward. If not, then he falls into the learned helplessness trap.

For example, if a student is getting a D in biology and feels that he really needs to buckle down to improve that grade, then studying harder becomes the solution. If the student studies day and night and really applies himself and still finds that he is getting a D he may be apt to stop studying since he is still getting the same grade. The feeling is that no matter what he does he is going to get a D so why put all this extra effort into something that he has no control over.

6. Plateau in performance – When you reach a level of performance that you've been striving for, you might back off a little. You become complacent with your performance – complacency is an athlete's nemesis. Things change, people change, you always have to be striving for new and better ways to do things. You don't want to become stagnant. If you keep doing what you've always done, you'll keep getting what you've always gotten. You can always reach a new plateau and discover new territory. The way to help combat this is to continually set new goals.
7. Fear of success – In this case, you are afraid of the perceived increased burden in regards to the expectations of others (i.e., more pressure, loss of privacy, higher expectations). The **change** is what is feared. People like things to stay status quo, change tends to bring on anxiety. With success, intrinsic motivation can get lost – you may need to take back

responsibility of your own intrinsic needs and realize that success is a personal thing. This fear of success can be seen by athletes who do extremely well, but falter just enough when it counts that they are edged out by someone else. In *Bring It On*, San Francisco 49er Merton Hanks tells about advice he once received from former 49er Eric Davis on not being fearful of success, and had this to say about fear, "90% of the defensive backs are scared of success, or are afraid to be successful. They're afraid to push themselves to be the best they can be" (Getts, 1996, p. 17).

Staying Motivated

You can help yourself and your team stay motivated by:

1. Goal Setting – Always keep in mind your individual and team goals. Goal setting will help keep your motivation and mental game at the level it should be all season long. Individual and team goal setting are strong motivational tools. The reason it is such a strong tool is that it takes away a lot of the uncertainty surrounding "How am I going to succeed at this level?" The goals provide that answer and give you the direction and confidence to move forward. This is centered around communication with your coach and teammates.
2. Positive Affirmation Statements – "I know I can do this," "I am a good hockey player," "I will achieve the goal I've set for myself today." If you find yourself having negative thoughts turn them around to something positive, right then and there. Relabeling negative thoughts as positive ones can be a very powerful tool.

3. Staying on an even keel – If you control your enthusiasm and your emotions, quiet intensity will be the result. Results aren't instant, you have to be committed for the duration. Trust that your actions will result in a certain outcome. It will just take patience and perseverance on your part. You need to stay on one level – no roller coaster rides!
4. Supporting each other – The presence of others practicing hard and performing well is contagious. Seeing teammates succeed not only increases motivation, but also breeds confidence. So, always make an effort to be supportive of one another.
5. Charting, recording and evaluating practice and progress are great motivational tools. Keep in mind though, progress has its up and downs. So don't get discouraged. Enjoy the process – the competition **and** the training. If you lose the enjoyment, then you lose a big part of your motivation.

Coaches and Motivation

Let's make something clear right here, coaches can not **make** someone be motivated. Self-motivation is a learned habit. The desires of self-motivators are internal, not external. You receive your gratification from meeting the internal goals you have set for yourselves, the ones that surpass winning. Those that are successful seem to posses a stronger desire to be successful. Understanding your needs, which are the basis for your goals, is very important when it comes to motivation. The desire to be successful, to be the best, and how that makes you feel, not how others view it, is what is important. You find a sense of security within yourself; and that means more than anything outsiders can give you. Coaches, you still need to praise these self-motivators too. Many times the self-motivators are left completely alone, almost like being punished because they are self-motivated. They need the attention just like the athletes that aren't as self-motivated.

There are several things for coaches to keep in mind when it comes to helping athletes maintain their motivation:

1. Positive reinforcement implemented immediately is the most powerful; yelling, intimidation and public humiliation are the least effective.
2. Maintain consistency, especially with new skills. You need to keep what works and change what doesn't until it becomes a new habit.
3. Respond to effort and behavior, not to performance outcome alone; reinforce change in the right direction.
4. Learning is not entirely cumulative – it has its ups and downs.
5. Vary practices to help avoid monotony. Have certain drill that are creative and fun. You need to find the joy in each drill as well. Have drills that are competitive and involve rewards (no running after practice) and have built-in penalties for not doing well (having to bring in the equipment after practice).
6. Do different things – have guest speakers, watch videos of other teams (for learning and motivational purposes), etc.
7. Allow athletes some say in their practice schedule. Keep in mind, a sense of perceived control is a powerful motivating factor and can make players more productive. Having choices that lie within the rules is a strong motivating catalyst. When athletes feel a sense of ownership in a decision, they tend to support it more strongly. You need to empower the athletes, this will increase their intrinsic motivation.
8. Make sure that their individual goals are compatible with the goals the team has set as a group.

9. Build in success to practice. Practice is a time to gain self-confidence not self-doubt. Mix in drills that you know they will yield 100% success.
10. Keep everyone active, don't give players a lot of time to stand around. Let players give some of their own practice ideas. Everyone should know the practice plan and their responsibilities for the day – it should be posted well before practice.
11. Always have a good "why." Why are we doing this drill? Why are we traveling to play that team? Why do we need to have team meetings every Tuesday after practice? Provide good solid answers to these questions.
12. Give a questionnaire pre-season to find out things about your athletes: How do they like to be motivated? After an error do they like to be approached? Left alone? Wait until after game? Why do they play? Types of rewards they like? What they like most about practice. What they like least.

Practice and Motivation

Motivation starts during practice. You need to practice all aspects of your game, not just what you are good at. Bob Quinn, Ex-General Manager, NY Yankees, Cincinnati Reds, SF Giants says, "There's always someone down at the minor leagues trying to take your job. It creates a certain amount of incentive, a certain amount of pressure to want to remain successful. As a result, those who stay focused and work on those things in which they are deficient, by and large succeed. So many want to work on things they are already proficient at, instead of working on those things they have the greatest amount of difficulty with." You need to make working hard on all aspects of your game a habit (a learned response or behavior).

Success becomes possible when technique, combined with pride and consistency, becomes habit. It is said that it takes a person 10 weeks to make a daily habit of an activity (Tutko & Tosi). It's easier to instill good habits than it is to break bad ones later on in your athletic career. Doing it wrong once makes it easier to do it that way again and again. Don't rush, this is your time to learn, there is no hurry. You want to get the technique right from the beginning so that you don't develop bad habits. Ask a lot of questions during practice, don't just make assumptions that may come back to haunt you later on. Take one day at a time, incremental change is the best way to go. When mistakes happen, admit it, see it as feedback to improve the future, and then do your best not to repeat them. Setbacks should be viewed as temporary.

"We are what we repeatedly do. Excellence, then, is not an act, but a habit." Aristotle

Human beings are creatures of habit, we tend to stick to our normal patterns of behavior, even if they aren't the correct ones. In practice, you need to use that time to change habits that aren't beneficial to you. You have to be persistent because it is very easy to fall back into old, comfortable patterns. It may take extra effort in the beginning, but it is definitely worth it. Change is temporary, and if you are consistent you will be able to move smoothly into the new behavior.

Keep in mind that the gap between what you want and actual results is caused by lack of action. You have the ultimate control over whether you are going to work hard all year. You are responsible, no one else, for your own actions. Whether you are going to hustle everyday during practice is a choice you make. Approach each practice and game with 100% commitment and effort. Realize that staying motivated during practice **every day** can be a difficult task, but it is crucial. Practice is the time to hone skills and form a solid foundation for success during games. Repetition is the best teacher.

Your mental and physical efforts during practice are direct indicators of how you will play in a game. Giving ½, or a token, effort during practice shows itself during games; you get in the habit of withholding some of your effort. Also, by not paying attention during practice you are more apt to develop bad habits if you're just going through the motions. Even on those days when you're hurt, drained, etc. and you only have 80% – you should give 100% of that 80% you have. Be patient during these times, there are always going to be occasions when your motivation is decreased for one reason or another. The right kind of practice must accompany the right kind of dedication. And remember, have fun. Isn't that the main reason you started in the first place?

Going all out in every drill helps develop the mental stamina you need for games. Remember, every drill has a purpose, you may not always see it, but it does. You may not think that each drill individually will make a difference, but the drills collectively can make the difference between winning and losing. "The typical athlete goes all out during competition ... the exceptional athlete goes all out to prepare for competition" (Dorfman & Kuehl, p. 105). The willingness to practice hard now, for a payoff down the road, is what sets apart a mediocre team from a great one. Keep in mind, last minute mental preparation is as effective as trying to teach a pitcher a new pitch to use in a game just 30 minutes prior to his start!

Game Day Motivation

It's vital that you treat conference games and non-conference games with the same intensity and motivation.

Find similarities between the two (i.e., you have the same defense as top team). Use non-conference or preseason games to implement new game strategies. This is also a time to stress individual goals. And, remember, every game starts out 0-0 and sports have seen more than its share of upsets.

Losing is going to happen, you need to learn that early on. Many times defeat forces you to take a long and hard look at where you are and where you want to be. So, just don't accept it, make changes to try to ensure it doesn't happen on a constant basis. Take a look at all the top teams, none of them are perfect all the time, the difference is that they didn't fall apart, they stayed focused and motivated in their quest to improve. Both winning and losing can be motivating if you know how to take the lessons presented from both. They both give you a chance to learn and grow from the experience.

Exercise #5

One thing that can help is to have post-game evaluations. Write down all the positive and negative thoughts and incidents. Go over the things that went well and be aware that those are the things you want to continue. Go over the negatives and make those a focus for the next week or so. If you need to discuss something with a coach or teammate, do so and then let it go. Let this post-game evaluation serve as motivation for future performances.

In summary, motivation is the state of mind that fuels the fire about achieving a goal. Being totally dedicated is what is going to keep you consistent in your actions so you can accomplish what you want. If you want to work towards and reach higher levels of performance, you must learn how to get the most out of your abilities. This will more likely come true if you are strongly motivated in the right direction. Your motivation will increase if: there is intrinsic pleasure derived from the sport, there are challenges, you are able to feel success, you feel you have some control and feel competent, and there is a positive social influence. And, it will decrease if: there is anxiety, failure, the influence of others is too important, you are only extrinsically motivated, you feel there is little or no control, and there is no feeling of competence or success. Motivation will be sustained if there is a perception of competence, a sense of pride in performance, as well as a feeling of control.

Ideally, you will see weaknesses as challenges to be worked on, and you won't lay any blame or make excuses. You will take responsibility for workout slumps and break the habit of finding excuses. You need to be motivated to do whatever it takes to reach your optimal level. Motivation requires responsibility, belief in oneself, maximum effort and coachability. When all is said and done, you are solely responsible for your own motivation. Your coaches, peers and family can help you in your quest to sustain that motivation, but the ultimate decision is yours.

Chapter 7
On a Mission

"Where there is no vision, people perish." Proverbs 29:18

Teams that perform at an optimal level on a consistent basis seem to be highly motivated by a sense of mission. This is different from having a goal, it's more than a goal - it's a team's collective sense of purpose. We each have our own mission for what we do. Athletes have a mission, coaches, owners, business men and women, corporations, work groups, etc. There's always something, down deep, a desire that pushes us to be successful in all of our endeavors. When being interviewed at the 1996 Summer Olympics in Atlanta, Carl Lewis said, "I enjoy the same thing now that I did as a child. My passion to win is no different now then 12 years ago." The desire to excel and attain the highest standards of performance in your sport is a commendable objective. But it will take commitment and sacrifice on your part, as well as enough self-control to withstand the adversity sports many times present. You can never lose sight of your dreams and aspirations.

Having a goal but no mission is almost like putting the cart before the horse. Unless you have a mission, a deep personal meaning of why you are doing what you are doing, you may not be **as** motivated to stick to your plan to reach the level of athleticism or excellence you are striving for. Once you clearly define your mission, your goals become the steps to actualizing your mission. Two-time

Olympian Marilyn King talks about aligning passion, vision and action, "Passion is the source of tremendous energy and creativity exhibited by peak performers. Vision is the art and science of how to use the mind to guide the daily effective action producing extraordinary results." You need to align the three into what Marilyn calls "Olympian Thinking." The athletes that possess all three of these are the elite ones.

You must have a clear picture in your mind of what you want, and then strongly believe that you can achieve it. This comes from having a strong awareness of yourself. You need to know the answer to the questions, "How important is it for me to excel in my sport?" and "Why is it so important for me to excel?" What are the needs and wants that my sport can fulfill? True competition comes from inside yourself, a strong fighting desire to excel. Your vision will be born out of your desire and hunger for success. From there you have to hold yourself accountable to the actions that will help you excel as you would like. This comes in the form of how you approach learning and improving on what you know at this point in time. With this you also need to understand that you will have to risk some setbacks along the way, and see this as part of the natural process to achieve greater things. People who succeed in life are those who can look at challenges positively and are able to make the necessary adjustments to put them on the right track.

What is a mission statement?

Unlike goals, which are specific and measurable, a mission statement is subjective. It's one team's, or one athlete's, personal reason(s) for playing their particular sport (or doing their particular job). It's having a strong, passionate belief in a personal philosophy that instills the basis for you to set your specific goals (Garfield, 1984). Your mission answers the questions, "Why am I doing this?" and "What does playing (i.e., football) mean to me?" It's finding out what generates that special drive which plays such an integral role for you to prevail in athletics. It's the intent and purpose of the team or individual. Your mission provides commitment and identification with the things you want to ultimately achieve. Once you define your mission, it will help tremendously in your motivation and it will aid you in charting a course of action. Your mission statement becomes the basis from which you make decisions. It becomes a yardstick for all that you do.

Examples of Mission Statements

- ➡ United States Olympic Training Center in Colorado Springs, Colorado, as stated on their brochure - "To serve as a visible symbol and commitment to its programs and the furtherance of the Olympic Movement in the United States."
- ➡ San Jose State University Softball team for the 1996 season - "We, the Spartan Softball team, believe that together we're better; and, united we stand, divided we fall" (as stated by then-head coach Debbie Nelson). This is the creed that motivated them to go out and perform day in and day out.
- ➡ San Francisco 49er Wide Receiver J.J. Stokes, "I play because I love to play, not because I can make a living out of it."
- ➡ The University of San Francisco Baseball team's mission for the 1996-7 season was "C.O.M.P.E.T.E.," and this stood for Combine Our Maximum Personal Effort for Team Excellence. Their mission the year before was M.A.G.I.C. Today, which stood for Make A Great Individual Commitment Today.

- ➡ Individual figure skater – "I skate because I love experiencing the thrill of accomplishing new things and then performing them in a competition."
- ➡ Individual runner's – "I like the feeling of pushing myself to the outer edge of my abilities."

Devising your mission statement

Now, how do you come up with an effective mission statement for your team? As a group, get together and brainstorm why it is you participate in your sport. It must be a collaborative effort. If there isn't any involvement in establishing it, there won't be any dedication in upholding it. Keep in mind, it's much deeper than, "I like it." "Knowing what really motivates you and keeping a crystal clear image of the goal is critical in sustaining energy over the long term," says 2-time Olympian Marilyn King. Think about what exactly it is that you like about it, and why it is you work so hard every day to become better.

- ➡ Is it the competition?
- ➡ The feeling of excelling at something few others can?
- ➡ The feeling of pushing yourself to the limit?
- ➡ The feeling of control?
- ➡ The personal challenge of wanting to do better than the year before?
- ➡ The desire to break records?
- ➡ Because you love the social aspect of it?
- ➡ The passion for the sport?
- ➡ Is it the one place you feel confident and at total peace with yourself?
- ➡ The prestige and attention?
- ➡ The scholarship you receive?

Exercise #6

Take some time, really think about it and then devise a list. The answers to these questions will most likely serve as your strongest motivation. You might want to look at players and teams you admire and see some of the characteristics that you like in them. Chances are they will be things you possess, or wish to posses. You need to find out what you want **your** niche to be, who you are and who you are not.

After everyone, individually, has come up with a few, write them on the board or a piece of paper. The process needs to include all the team members and be a collaborative effort. This is important, so take as much time as necessary, don't rush the process. Then, as a unanimous group, decide on the top three and consolidate them into one statement – something everyone agrees on and feels can serve as a motivator each and every day. "We play hockey because ..." or an acronym that suits your team, or whatever you like. This mission will help bond the team and it will be the thing you always come back to. It's a psychological contract among the members of the team.

Keep your mission statement visible – put it on a t-shirt, a poster in the locker room, in everyone's locker, write it on your wrist band, put it in your hat, in your room – wherever you prefer. Have it so that it functions as a constant reminder of why you're out there working hard all the time. On those days when it seems like a real effort, or chore, to be at practice, for whatever reason, that's the time to read it more than once. It provides the reason why you should give that extra effort. ***You wrote it, you live by it.***

After you create a team mission, you need to devise your own personal mission statement that complements the team's. Your mission provides direction, momentum and builds ownership to your vision. It is up to each individual player to uphold the principles of your mission. Don't let day-to-day frustrations slow you down. Remember, the team with a strong mission statement, one that everyone believes in wholeheartedly, is the one that's going to excel. That's the team that is going to reach deep down and find a way to succeed ***every day***, not just in the clutch situations. Teams that lack a clear mission statement don't always play up to their potential. "Having the talent is the easy part, you know you need it. You need that passion, that's what makes people like Rice so good, that passion is so deep and so heavy," says former San Francisco 49er Tight End, Dr. Jamie Williams.

"The future belongs to those who believe in the beauty of their dreams." Eleanor Roosevelt

You need to have a dream, then back it with your passion and dedication and follow up with a concrete plan of action. Your mission establishes your priorities for you to work with. You must have the passion and commitment to yourself, your teammates and to your sport. Without a strong sense of mission and a strong focus, people deviate from the plan. You have to love your sport and be willing to go the extra mile. Your mission provides the extra motivation to do just that.

Put your mission first in terms of what you **should** do as opposed to what you **want** to do at a given time. Always act in accordance with fulfilling your mission. If you are tempted to go out with friends the night before a game, think to yourself, is this behavior in accordance with my mission and goals? "Devotion to self-improvement is more apt to bring results than devotion to self-adulation" (Dorfman & Kuehl, p. 44). Keep in mind the kind of player you want to be and the kind of team you want to be a part of. And then think – do I want to take a chance? Act with integrity, that is, don't allow your values or talents to be compromised in any way, shape or form. There comes a point where you have to take a stand and be devoted to all that you believe in and persevere, no matter what. San Francisco 49ers Vice President/Director of the 49ers Foundation, Lisa DeBartolo, talks about the 49ers sense of mission and that they, "adhere to the principle that they're not going to stand for anything that isn't first class." You need to separate needs from wants, and do what "needs" to be done first. The ongoing validity of your mission must also be examined to make sure you are going in the right direction.

In summary, a mission statement is a personal statement or creed representing why it is you do what you do. Every team **needs** to have a mission, a reason for being. It is what is going to be the fire that keeps the team working and achieving together. Each player's personal mission statement will help them individually stay pursuant of the things that will make them better athletes, and in turn contribute immensely to the team. Your mission statement is going to set the tone for everything you do – so make sure you're comfortable with it and wholeheartedly believe in it.

"Cherish your vision and your dreams as they are the children of your soul – the blueprints of your ultimate achievements." Napoleon Hill

Chapter 8
Goal Setting

Now that we've talked about devising a mission statement for you and your team; it's time to move on to the next step – turning that vision into a reality. You have to develop goals that go hand-in-hand with that mission – starting with your long-term goal. When setting goals the succession of events goes like this: set a goal, have a detailed plan, commit to that plan, and then take action. Sound easy? It can be if you take goal setting seriously and approach it systematically.

Outcome versus performance goals

Most athletes say that their goal is to win. Winning, of course, is the objective, but the key to goals is that they are in your control, and winning is not always within your direct control, especially in team sports. If you play hard and smart, and focus on specific areas within your control, winning will take care of itself. When you are more concerned about the outcome than the process you are, ironically, decreasing your chances of seeing that happen. By keeping your focus on the process you are taking the emphasis off the outcome; and as a result, you will feel less pressure to win.

It's more effective to set performance goals as opposed to outcome goals. Athletes like to set outcome goals because we are conditioned by society that winning equals a good performance, though many of us know first hand that this is not always the case. We are led to believe that second best isn't good enough by statements such as "better luck next time" and "too bad you didn't win." At the Olympics you hear (many times) how an athlete lost the gold, instead of how they won the silver. Just participating in the Olympics is a big accomplishment and makes you a success and a winner, and should be viewed as such.

Keep in mind, winning is not the **only** objective, it's more than that, it's the enhancement of your self-image and the fulfillment of your dreams. Winning has to be a personal thing of you achieving the goals that you have set for yourself. Don't lose sight of the fact that reaching a personal goal carries its own reward. It is overcoming any obstacles to reach your goal. The value of winning is only as great as the value of the goal you set and obtained. Real success is in your own mind, not in the minds of others or measured by monetary compensation. Success then becomes defined by the standards you have established for yourself, not other peoples definition; and, is the achievement of **your** own performance goals that are aligned with **your** ability level. Your personal victories must come before any public victories (Covey, 1990). Bear in mind, success in any area of your life is contingent on you setting goals and is a by-product of hard work and persistence. In the words of Vince Lombardi, "Winning isn't everything, but making the effort to win is."

Long-term goals

A long-term goal is an objective statement about a specific achievement that can be measured. What is it the team ultimately wants to accomplish? Or, what is it I ultimately want to achieve? An example of this would be "to finish .500 **or above** at the end of season," or "to have a fielding percentage of **at least** .945 at the end of the season." When most players are asked what their goal is they typically reply, "I want to win," "Play in the pros," or "Be the best." These statements tell you little on how to achieve this and they don't direct your behavior. It is very important for the team, coaches and individual players to have a long-term goal in mind. Approach your long-term goal incrementally – one game at a time, one practice at a time, one short-term goal at a time – otherwise it may seem too overwhelming and out of reach. Place all your efforts and energy into achieving this goal. Keeping in mind, "What is it I need to do to attain my definitive goal?" If you are not sure of numbers, a suggestion is to look at the numbers from last year, as well as the numbers of the team that won the league/conference and make a realistic assessment that way. San Francisco 49er Jerry Rice refers to goals in terms of having a spiraling goal to be better than the year before. So, last year's numbers set the standard for the following year (Crumpacker, p. C-7). Here are some examples of long-term goals:

- **At least** 20 wins next season.
- A team fielding percentage of .965 **or better**.
- As a team, have **at least** 6 hits per game.
- As a quarterback, have **at least** an average of 180 total passing yards per game.
- An earned run average of **no more than** 4.0 in conference games.
- **At least** 30 stolen bases this season.
- An on-base percentage of **at least** .875.
- Field goal percentage of .945 **or better** for the 1999 season.
- An average of **at least** 3 goals scored per game.
- Lead-off man retired **at least** 80% for this season.

One problem that teams tend to have is that they set long-term goals at the beginning of the season, then never go back to see how they are doing, and they don't really talk about their goals or strategies to get there. Former San Francisco 49er, Dr. Jamie Williams says, "Every team in the league will say they want to win the Super Bowl, but the 49ers take steps and strategies to achieve that goal, positive strategies. All things are pointed in the direction of that goal, that is why they are there." There must be consensus among the team in regards to the team goals, as well as an ongoing, periodic review and assessment of the goals so that they don't lose their effectiveness. Goals need to be clear and committed to by everyone involved, they need to act as one unit not as independents; since teams operate in an environment that requires cooperative work.

Short-term goals

From there you need to devise a series of short-term goals that have a high probability of success. "Accomplish the great task by a series of small acts" (Mitchell, p. 63). Your short-terms goals must be:

- ✔ Realistic – Your goals need to be progressively more challenging but achievable. You want to be able to experience success so that you'll be motivated to reach for the next goal. In addition, you will grow more confident with each realistic goal you accomplish. If they are continually too difficult this can lead to lack of confidence and motivation. Goal setting should be a positive source of motivation, not something that frustrates you because you keep falling short of your goals.
- ✔ Specific – A philosopher once said, "If you don't know where you are going – any road will get you there." You need to identify specific ways in which

you want to improve your game. Vague goals are like bad direction, you may eventually get there, but chances are it won't be the most direct or efficient route. Instead of "work on long field goals," a more accurate goal would be, "4 **or more** successful field goals from **at least** 40 to 50 yards 4 **or more** times this week."

- ✔ Action-oriented – "I want to be a starter" doesn't specify what you need to do to accomplish that. You can **want** all you want – but you need to act. You need to set goals regarding specific skills that are weaknesses and may be keeping you from a starting position. Action goals confine your thoughts, increase persistence, direct your focus and leave no room for distractions. It gives you control over the situation.
- ✔ Measurable – Ideally, you want to measure them objectively (with numbers), but if not, it can be done subjectively by you and your coach. For example, if your goal is to be "more aggressive" you and your coach need to break that down and identify behaviors that "more aggressive" means to both of you. This gives a clear cut way to compare actual performance versus desired performance within a framework you both agree on.
- ✔ Time-bound – When your goals are time-sensitive they have more of a motivational impact. If you leave it open you won't be as persistent in your pursuit. When you assign a target date to finish something, this will also aid in your ability to manage your time properly.

In addition, it is best to word your goals in a positive manner. It's not a good idea to use words like "don't" in your goal statements. They will most likely direct your attention to what it is you are trying to avoid ("Don't strike out"), as opposed to what you want to do. Here are some examples of short-term goals:

- ➡ By the first conference game, I'm going to improve my batting average to **at least** .278.
- ➡ At next week's game I'm going to rush for **at least** 80 yards.
- ➡ For the next game, I am going to get on base 2 times **or more**.
- ➡ This week at practice I am going to work on being more aggressive in my baserunning. This entails reading the pitcher better, working on my lead, running hard and working on my slide.
- ➡ I'm going to make 5 assist **or more** at next week's game.
- ➡ 18 pitches **or less** per inning in the conference game this weekend.

"Some people think it is easy to hit .300 because you fail 7 of 10 times. It looks easy but it's very difficult. So you say, 'Somehow, some way I'm going to put the ball in play and I'm going to get ***at least*** *one or two hits today.' Those are the people that are successful."* Bob Quinn, Ex-General Manager, NY Yankees, Cincinnati Reds, SF Giants

Your short-term goals should answer the question – "What do I need to do to see my long-term goal come to fruition?" These short-term goals provide you with the feedback necessary for you to know if you are on the right track. In *USA Weekend*, Florence Griffith Joyner has this to say about goal setting, "Setting goals is like driving a car, I never get in my car unless I know where I want to go. I set goals to take me places. Once I reach a goal, I set new ones" (Joyner, 1996 p. 6). Short-term goals are the stepping stones towards actualizing your mission and securing your commitment. Successful teams concern themselves daily with the short-term and get the most out of each training session.

Think of each short-term goal as a rung on a ladder – you don't go from the bottom to the top in one giant step; you must be patient and take one rung at a time. (And, make sure you are climbing the "right" ladder!) You must take action to get the results you desire. Take responsibility and focus on the here and now. Stay in the moment and only focus on the goal you have set for that day. By achieving each short-term goal, you will experience success, thus increasing your intrinsic motivation and self-confidence. Remember, it's the present that gets you to the future. Your long-term goal isn't going to be realized unless you back it up with a step-by-step plan of action that you stay dedicated to.

You can also think of each short-term goal like a piece of a puzzle. Once you put all the pieces together you should have the long-term goal you were striving for. You must see a connection between your daily and long-term goals. Sometimes there will be some short-term discomfort so that you can obtain greater gains in the future. You may have to take a step backwards, or stay put, before you can make great leaps and bounds in the direction you would like. Many times, the people who try to go too fast are actually doing themselves a disservice in the long run. **There is no such things as a short-cut**. People who take short-cuts always show it at some point in their career. They break down technically or mentally in some area that they rushed through when acquiring the skill. You need to evolve slowly and thoroughly as a complete athlete. "Deliberate and slow cultivation ... is the path to success and good fortune," I Ching no. 53. Sometimes it is hard to see the collective efforts of many individual tasks, but you need to keep in mind that they are all in line with what you are ultimately trying to achieve. We live in a society where we want instant results and instant gratification, but you must realize that you may have to give up something in the present to obtain something better in the future.

"The final destination is nothing compared to the journey, so don't be in a hurry!"

When setting any kind of goals it is important that you don't put a ceiling on your goal or become complacent when you achieve a goal. That is why it is good to use terms like "**at least**," "**or above**" and "**or more**" when goal setting. Your point of reference should be continuous improvement. This way you will always be striving for more - your goals should always define **minimum** performance. Never relax your determination and attitude toward being successful. These open-ended goals allow you to achieve extraordinary things. **Don't set limits, set goals**. Goal setting helps deal with and avoid complacency. You can feel good about what you've accomplished; but don't stop there, you need to keep setting higher goals. Don't slack off or start changing the things that have helped you reach your goals to this point (work ethic, conditioning, etc). Anytime you stop striving to get better, you will, most likely, get worse. You can always improve, if you feel you have all the answers, then you are imposing false limits on yourself. Here's an example, if a softball player says that she wants to get 2 hits at the next game, and if after her second at-bat she has those two hits, she might be inclined to say, "Well, I achieved my goal for the day, I can relax now." Whereas, if she says "**at least** 2 hits" then she will keep striving for more even after the first 2 hits.

This is also good to keep in mind when you are playing a game you view as "unimportant." (Although, all games should be viewed as equally important!). By always setting goals, the probability of losing motivation for games against less talented (or nonconference) teams will decrease since you have set your own goals to be focusing on. Many times when the competition is too easy you don't get to see the full potential of an athlete because they are out there giving only ½ of their effort. When, in reality, they should still be giving their all and trying to improve their **own** game.

You need to be dedicated mentally and physically to achieving the goals you've set for yourself. Follow these steps to help you with that:

1. Write down your goals – Clearly define what the results are that you desire. Once you know exactly where you're headed and what you expect to achieve, commit your objective to paper and verbalize it to someone (coach, teammate, parent, friend). This reinforces your sense of mission and devotion. Writing your goals down will help increase your dedication. Then, write down your progress in relation to the goals to use as feedback and motivation. Goals are a very powerful tool if used correctly.
2. Develop specific strategies – Decide on the plan that will most efficiently accomplish your short-term goals; i.e., the number of **quality** ground balls each practice, number of strikeouts for the next game, etc. Write it down and be specific. Remember, it's quality not quantity! The path you define must be very clear cut and precise.
3. When devising your series of goals, use the divide and conquer rule. Divide monumental tasks into short-term goals. They will be more manageable and easier to reach; and, as you accomplish each one, you will enjoy positive reinforcement and a feeling of success.

4. Prioritize your goals, don't try to do too many things at once. Just assume responsibility for the goal you are working on at the moment - don't overwhelm yourself. Then, start working on an area where the slightest of improvement will be visible, this will help you stay committed to your goal setting.
5. Once you set your goal you need to sit down and plan out how you are going to achieve it, mentally and physically. One way to do this is by having a goal card - see Table 1.

TABLE 1

Where Am I Now?	**Mid-way Goal**	**Long-Term Goal**
Batting Average of .203	**at least** .250	**at least** .300
Strategies to get me there	**Mentally**	**Physically**
	Visualize hitting well every day Daily goal setting Circle breathing at every at-bat	Work on outside pitch for an additional 10 pitches every day Increase batting practice by 5 mins

First, you need to realistically assess where you are now and take into consideration what your current capabilities are. Then, decide what your long-term goal is. Halfway between the two becomes your mid-season (mid-career) goal. From there your mental and physical strategies/plans become your short-term goals that you work on a daily basis.

6. To keep up with daily goal setting have a box at practice/game where you put your goal that you've made for that day. At the end of the day, you note on the card whether the goal was achieved, and if not, why? Some goals will be ongoing goals, things that will be worked on all week, all season, etc. There should also be periodic assessments of your goal card with your coach(es) to evaluate your progress. This increases commitment and allows for revision of goals when necessary.
7. It's important that you keep your goals in line with things you have control over. You can control your effort and the task you are working on; you can't control other people or the situation around you. If you focus only on things within your control you will be less susceptible to distractions.
8. Keep a positive and healthy attitude about your sport. Remember, no one is perfect. We all have bad days, but don't let that destroy or hamper your motivation. Setbacks are inevitable. Always keep in mind your goals and objectives. If you do this every day, at the end of the season you will be able to be proud of what you've done, knowing that you did something each day to help you reach your goals. Don't forget . . . the journey of 1,000 miles begins with 1 step.
9. Give credit where credit is due – Each day, congratulate yourself for completing the goal you set for that day (or the progress you've made on a certain goal). Enjoy the feeling of having taken another step towards your long-term goal.
10. Own your goals – For you to have the desire to take action you must own your goals and be committed to them. That's why it is so important for **you** to set your

own goals. Your goals need to be your own, either set only by you, or in collaboration with your coach. You know best what you want and need to do. From there you need to internalize your goals so that they are a part of who you are, and where you want them to take you. Be passionate about your goals and be accountable for them. You must be consistent and follow through with your goal setting.

11. Assess each new goal you make – Do my goals fit the guidelines (realistic, specific, etc.)? Am I willing to do what it takes to reach the goals I have set for myself? Do my daily/short-term goals go succinctly with my mid-season and long-term goals? How much control do I have over reaching my goals? Are there other ways of reaching my goals?

Benefits of goal setting

➡ Improves the quality of practice and performance
➡ Clarifies expectations
➡ Increases motivation and helps sustain motivation over a long period of time
➡ Relieves boredom by making training more challenging
➡ Increases pride and satisfaction
➡ Directs attention to the task at hand
➡ Helps put things in proper perspective
➡ Mechanism for building self-confidence
➡ Removes anxiety about feeling that you can't accomplish something
➡ Encourages you to be persistent in your pursuit

To be successful and productive the team must know what its goals and objectives are, both as a team and individually. No one person can do the job alone.

Productivity will be visible if both are established. Having a common goal, one that is agreed upon by everyone, not only makes the team more cohesive but also motivates the team to be productive and work even harder to be successful to achieve its goals and objectives. Working hard with your team leads to the realization of both your individual goals and the goals set by the team. Commitment to the goal is the glue that holds the team together, and it also involves sacrifice, cooperation and hard work. Clearly defining the goals of a team plays an integral part in being successful. The coordination of players so that their roles become complementary to the goals the team is striving to accomplish is crucial to successful team performance (Cartwright & Zander). This can be done during the initial team meeting at the beginning of the season. Once the team goals have been set, the players can then proceed to set corresponding individual goals.

Everything you do as a team, you need to do as an individual player. By each player setting and working toward their individual goals, they are, in the same effort, helping the team achieve its collective goal. Individual goals are enhanced by team goals. Here's an example of an individual's **long-term** goal: "to hit **at least** .298 by the end of the season." And, here's an example of another individual's **short-term** goal: "I will increase my game foul shooting percentage from 43% to **at least** 60% by September 5th." Both of these goals will not only help the individual, but also the team as well – it's a win/win situation for everyone.

In summary, goals are going to provide the direction and motivation to actualizing your mission. Approach your goals systematically – set your long-term goal and work backwards from there. Where should I be mid-way through?, next week? Then go to your daily goals. Set goals outside of sports as well. These techniques are applicable in any area of your life – sports, social, work, family, school and personal improvement. They help you grow, change and improve. Remember, goal setting requires thoughtful and systematic effort for you to achieve what you've set out for. Don't be in a hurry, work on one goal at a time, and you'll soon be able to look back and see how far you've come.

Chapter 9
Stress and Relaxation

"Relax!" "Relax!" That's what your coach says to do, right? But how is this possible with the bases loaded, the game on the line and you at bat; or, the game tied in overtime with you going out to kick a field goal. Before we get into the actual relaxation techniques, it's important to talk about tension, stress and anxiety; all the things that cause us to be in dire need of relaxation skills. Stress is a big part of everyone's life, and we all need a slight level of stress (eustress) to push us, but too much **perceived** stress can be a problem. Too much stress will cause a team to break down, or at the minimum, be more susceptible to break down. This chapter will address what stress is, how it manifests itself as well as physical and mental ways to reduce anxiety and tension during practice or games. As well as teach you breathing techniques to help your relax and relieve tension.

What is stress?

Stress can be defined as an imbalance between what you perceive is being demanded of you from the environment and what you deduce your capabilities are when you perceive the outcome to be important. Stress becomes a factor when the external or internal demands are appraised as exceeding the resources of the person (Ungerleider & Golding, 1992). A situation doesn't become stressful until it is interpreted negatively. In other words, nothing has a good or bad meaning until you give it meaning based on your perceptions. Feelings of being under pressure is something that is self-created, again, based on your perception of the surrounding circumstances. If you are attending to only the relevant cues that are necessary to successfully complete your task, you won't feel like you are under so much pressure. So, at the most basic level, stress is a result of a person's negative thoughts in response to environmental stimulus compounded by arousal. When that arousal increases to the point where relevant cues are eliminated, that is when performance will be negatively effected.

When you are seemingly stressed, anxious and have feelings of apprehension, this will be accompanied by a heightened level of physiological arousal. Your blood flow and your hormones are dramatically influenced by how you perceive a situation. Increased arousal affects you mentally and physically (i.e., an anxious quarterback will tense up, his visual field narrows, and he throws an interception). Arousal perceived as negative or positive is the key to anxiety. Anxiety will stimulate your fight or flight response. Physically, your body is preparing to increase your chances of survival and to help you to deal with perceived life-threatening situations. Physiologically, the following things are effected:

1. There is an increase in: sympathetic nervous system activity, body metabolism, heart rate, brain wave activity, pupil dilation, blood sugar level, blood pressure, adrenalin, breathing rate, oxygen consumption, and muscular tension.
2. There is a decrease in: visual field, blood flow and flexibility. You may encounter coordination losses, and since there is no fluid motion you may experience the "death grip." Energy level is also decreased due to the fact that you are contracting your muscles for an

extended period of time, which leads to premature fatigue. That's why it is so important to keep your nonworking muscles loose.

Psychologically, there are many things that are affected due to an increase in arousal and stress:

- ✔ Reduced concentration – Due to the increased mental activity and reduced visual field, it is very hard to focus on the relevant cues to be able to perform your particular job well. Due to the narrowing of perceptual field and inability to attend to necessary cues you are unable to detect danger signals and external cues that are imperative for you to execute your task effectively.
- ✔ Worry – Negative thoughts that lead to stress take the form of worry. Worry lies at the root of tension, it engenders anxiety and focuses on the undesirable and negative "what if?" When you start worrying and doubting yourself, you increase your anxiety level. Under stress, negative thoughts become more believable and the focus of your attention.
- ✔ Feeling overwhelmed and confused – This is due to the increased brain wave activity. Your mind is racing much too fast for you to be productive, which can cause you to just "freeze" because your body doesn't quite know what to do. I remember as a skater forgetting my routine during big competitions because I was nervous and overwhelmed. "You have to be able to deal with your nerves and overcome it. You can't go out there and freak out. That's the nature of the business, it's not so much physical, it's all mental," says former San Francisco 49er Kicker Jeff Wilkins.
- ✔ No feeling of control – With added anxiety you feel as if your back is to the wall and you don't have

complete control over the situation you are in. This then leads to a lack of confidence. Bear in mind, there are some things that are out of your control (weather, bad calls, etc.), and you need to accept this!

- ✔ Feeling of helplessness – After seeing the cycle of tension and negative performances you may just give up due to a sense of dread and helplessness.
- ✔ Decision making – Given the fact that you may not be able to process information in a productive manner, your ability to properly make decisions may be temporarily impaired. You may make premature decisions, not look at all the facts or be able to think through all of your options clearly. Or, your judgement may just be "off."

Sources of stress

- ✔ Fear of failure and resulting social disapproval – You need to concern yourself with the task at hand, not the consequences. When you're constantly worrying about failure and disapproval you are just increasing your chances of that happening due to all the negative physiological and psychological changes that go along with increased anxiety. Dwelling on fears makes them seem more real and likely to come true.
- ✔ Injury and overtraining – High anxiety increases your chances of injury due to you being insecure and cautious in your movements. Also, constantly reacting with a stressful response will lower your resistance to illness and injury. You are more likely to get hurt when tired and tense, especially when coordination is disrupted and movements are only committed to halfway. It's important to monitor your stress level to help prevent injury.

- ✔ Life-stressors – Anything labeled as a life-stressor (death of spouse or family member, divorce, sudden financial change) increases your risk of injury, based on an increase in muscle tension and deficits in attention during these times.
- ✔ Your perception of the situation and perceived lack of ability – If you feel the competition is extremely important and/or that you are in way over your head, this can be a big stressor unless you are able to realistically assess the situation, your current abilities, and put things in the proper perspective.
- ✔ Equating self-worth with performance – You are not your performance! Your self-worth is stable, while your performance may vary from time to time. Internal demands can be stressful if they threaten self-esteem. When you perceive that you won't be successful in meeting the performance demands and feel a strong threat to your self-esteem, this will most likely trigger your stress reaction.

Burnout

If not handled correctly, all of the above can lead to burnout. Burnout is physical and mental exhaustion, resulting in a lack of interest in your sport. The fun factor is nowhere to be found and now it's more like a chore. It's a sense of distress, discontent and perception of failing to achieve the mission/goals that you have set. The cost now outweighs the rewards. The stress usually comes from disrespect from teammates/coaches, not feeling that you make an impact, frustration and fatigue because your devotion and efforts haven't produced the results you wanted. It's a problem born of good intentions (Martens, 1987). Some ways to deal with burnout are:

1. Reassess goals – Are your goals realistic? Do you have the resources necessary to achieve these goals?

You need to acknowledge that having to change a goal isn't failing. It takes a smart and resourceful person to know when it is time to reset a goal, rather than risk burnout, injury, etc.

2. Maintain a strong support system – Lean on those that are close to you, that is what they are there for. Instead of keeping things inside, bend their ear when you feel the urge. You'll feel better after having done so.
3. Acknowledge your humanness and time constraints – Only so much can be done in a day, it's the quality of what you do, not the quantity. Keep quality high and train efficiently.
4. Take care of yourself physically and mentally – You can't be an effective athlete, coach, or executive, if you aren't up to the day-in and day-out challenges mentally or physically. To be the most productive for those around you, you need to take care of yourself first. You also need the awareness of when your body needs rest, because without the proper rest your mind-body system will falter or shut down.
5. Balance your life with alternate activities – Take time off from your primary sport now and then, but still participate in sports to keep you mentally and physically sharp. For example, a basketball player might play golf in the off-season to keep his fine motor skills tuned; or a football player may play basketball to keep his body conditioned.

You need to find your own way of preserving physical, mental and spiritual equilibrium. When you are calm and relaxed even the most taxing of tasks will seem easy. Some methods to deal with and reduce stress both cognitively and behaviorally are:

1. Make a list of all issues that make you stressed.

2. Assess each situation by reading through to see what can be done with each (if anything). See which ones may be beyond your control.
3. Provide structure and devise a game plan to deal with the ones within your control.

If you find that some of them are within your control, you can alter your responses to the situations by the following:

1. Alter the meaning/appraisal of stress by taking away the importance of the situation. If you treat every situation with the same strategy, this will not only provide consistency with your coping mechanisms, but also reduce your stress level due to having an even-keeled approach and attitude.
2. Focus on the situation not the consequences. Be aware of what you are doing and what you can be doing regarding the task at hand. Be process-oriented, not results-oriented and focus on the present.
3. Control your feelings and emotional responses. Be aware of the self-talk you use and monitor if it is helping or hurting. Relabel certain feelings so that your perception will be positive not negative. For example, relabel being "keyed-up" (negative connotation) as "excitement" (positive connotation), thus reducing your stress level.
4. When possible, change the environment you are in. If certain venues are anxiety producing, change the venue if possible. If not, go to the venue when there isn't a competition so that you can get used to being in those surroundings so you will be more comfortable the next time you are there.
5. Smiling, laughing and music can also be used to help reduce mental stress. San Francisco 49er Defensive Back, Marquez Pope, says that the beat of the music serves as a trigger for him to relax.

6. All exercise (if kept in proper perspective) reduces stress. A fit body is able to withstand the internal wear-and-tear that occurs under stress. Exercise is a natural tranquilizer. A sustained period of exercise causes secretion of endorphins, which results in what is called a "runner's high."
7. Relaxation techniques

Relaxation

Being in a relaxed state is important to achieving optimal performance in any endeavor, not just sports. It's important when you're taking a test, giving a presentation, having a job interview, dealing with your children, etc. You name it, being relaxed will increase your productivity in it. It is a vital stepping stone to peak performance. If you're not relaxed, everything you do will be a struggle. Relaxation provides a mind-body integration necessary for peak performance.

You can use relaxation skills at all stages of practice – beginning, during and end. At the beginning as a way to get your mind clear and your body relaxed so you can get the most out of the practice session. During practice, you can use breathing skills to regain focus and slow your body down. And, at the end of practice as part of cooling down to help you return to a balanced physical state. Relaxation and breathing skills help improve your circulation (blood flow), which can help reduce the risk of injury and allows your body to get back to its normal state in a speedier fashion.

Benefits

➡ Improves concentration ability – It will help you in your ability to tune out distractions and gives you better sensory awareness.

- ➡ Improves body awareness – You need to know when you are under or over aroused. When learning this the coach can help by giving feedback to the player if he sees him being overly aroused (tense) or under aroused (lethargic).
- ➡ Speeds up healing time following an injury – The body needs to recover fully if it's going to perform at an optimal level in the near future.
- ➡ Learning is enhanced – Research shows that after a certain period of time the learning process peaks and any additional instruction may confuse and/or undo progress made. By interspersing periods of learning with relaxation sessions you will absorb more without any deterioration of learning (Syer & Connolly). Also, it is much easier to introduce new thoughts and ideas when your mind is clear and you are relaxed. Skills are best learned when you are in a relaxed state and there is an absence of tension.
- ➡ Shuts down rational mind – This allows you to perform more instinctually and intuitively without having to deal with all the chatter that may take place in your head when you are stressed.
- ➡ Helps you sleep better
- ➡ Increases flexibility
- ➡ Strengthens abdominal muscles
- ➡ Assists in releasing errors
- ➡ Energizes you by giving oxygen to your muscles
- ➡ Helps get your rhythm back
- ➡ Puts your focus back on the present task at hand and gives you a sense of control
- ➡ Prepares you for a productive practice session
- ➡ Helps control anxiety and arousal level
- ➡ Prepares you for mental imagery

I am going to go over two basic relaxation techniques – circle breathing and a progressive relaxation session. These skills are necessary to perform at an optimal level in athletics, and they are the same sort of skills that are taught in stress management classes for businesses, and can be used in any facet of your life. It's important to note that the days of pep talks to psych up your team are over. Rigid, tight-jawed determination is not the key, a sense of relaxation and letting go is. During the track events at the Summer Olympics the commentators made note of how some of the runners looked so tense (their shoulders were being held higher and their facial muscles were tight). And, needless to say, these were not the athletes that went on to win. The athlete/team that is mentally and physically relaxed and has "quiet intensity" is the one that is going to come out on top.

Circle Breathing

Circle breathing is a great on-the-spot tool for athletes. Right before you throw a pitch, shoot a free throw, swing the bat, field a ball, kick a field goal – all these tasks require great concentration and focus. The breathing will help you be better prepared and allow you to keep your poise in tough situations. You are better able to read your environment if you are calm and relaxed. Mental poise and emotional control are key to you performing well and being successful.

The center of your body is right behind your belly button, and this is where you want to start your breath from. Starting from there (the center of your body), draw air in slowly through your nose, all the way up to your chest for a count of 4, hold it for a count of 2, then slowly exhale through your mouth for a count of 4. Let go of all tension and old energy, and completely clear your mind.

Focus only on your breathing. That is one deep breath. Approximately 5-10 of these in a row will help get you into a more relaxed state. Now, stop here and try to do a few deep breaths on your own before moving on. Go at your body's pace, it will tell you when to take another breath.

Progressive Relaxation

In the 1930s, Edmund Jacobson demonstrated that you can't be on opposite ends of the physiological and emotional spectrum (Tutko & Tosi). That is, an anxious mind cannot exist in a relaxed body; or, a quiet mind can not exist in a tense body. He introduced Progressive Muscle Relaxation. This entails tensing each muscle, holding it and then relaxing each muscle on the exhale. It's a loosening up and letting go mentality. The letting go lets you know what absence of tension feels like. This type of relaxation skill gives you a heightened awareness of when and how you experience tension, this can then serve as a cue that you should do something to relieve the tension. You need to be able to communicate with your body and understand what it is trying to tell you.

Guidelines for relaxation sessions

1. It is best to do your relaxation session at the same time every day (i.e., before practice/game and before you go to bed). Providing this consistency is very important because regular practice is essential if you want to reap the full benefits.
2. It's best if you have someone talk you through a scripted relaxation session the first few times until you become more familiar with it. Then you can do it yourself, or make a tape and play it whenever you want to do a relaxation session.

3. Find a quiet, comfortable place to relax, make sure you don't have any constricting clothing on and don't do it after you have just eaten a meal.
4. You can lay down, as long as you don't feel you will fall asleep. If that is the case, then sit up until you have disciplined yourself enough to lay down and remain awake. Sorry, sleeping does not equal practicing relaxation skills!
5. Completely clear your mind of anything else. Now is the time to focus only on your breathing. At this point in time there is nothing more important than this relaxation session.

Start off with 5-10 deep breaths. Then, when you have taken all the proper measures to prepare yourself for a productive session, start with your feet and tense them as tight as possible and hold for a count of 4, then let go and have all the tension leave your feet, imagining all the tension and stress slowly leaving both your feet (this is on the exhale). Then, move on to your calves, again tensing them for a count of 4, then releasing all the tension from them. And, do the same for your thighs, buttocks, stomach, chest, hands, forearms, biceps, shoulders, back, neck, and facial muscles. All the while you should be doing your circle breathing.

Do a quick body scan and see if there is any tension left in your body. If you tend to carry your tension in your feet, then there is a chance that you will still be tense there. So, this is the time when you need to go back to that place and tense and relax these muscles again and again until you feel completely relaxed. When you are done, your whole body should feel sort of limp. This process should take about 20 minutes (10-15 after you have honed the skill). Take note, some athletes feel that this is not the best technique to do right before practice or a game because it gets them too relaxed. It's a trial and error approach, as with your physical skills, use practice as your forum to first try this.

Now, we all need some level of arousal to perform, it is said that every athlete needs to be aroused to a level slightly above resting state, the key is how much above? Each one of you will differ here. The object is to assess how you react in stressful situations so that you can find a way to counter this, it is not a time to judge yourself for your reactions, or label them as good or bad. Be realistic in your assessment – this is the only way to help improve your performance. The key is finding the balance between relaxation and readiness and finding out your level of bad/good/optimal arousal.

Exercise #7

Go back to the section **Sources of stress** (page 134-5) and put a star next to the ones you feel are applicable to you. Then, think about times when you have been stressed, what are the tell-tale signs that you are, in fact, "stressed?" Are there physiological changes? If so, what are they? Psychological changes? If so, what are they? Then, think about what alterations you can make after looking at the list you created. Can you use relaxation skills, reduce the importance of competition, alter your self-talk? This is a good way to find out how you manifest stress. You also might want to refer back to the exercise you did in Chapter 6 regarding your optimal arousal level to help you with this exercise.

Breathing techniques are so simple that I think they are many times overlooked. These are such powerful tools, yet many players have yet to buy in and take the time to perfect these skills. The team that is educated about stress and its impact on performance, and are able to recognize and control their own arousal states is the team that is going to be the most successful. They are the ones that are able to keep their wits about themselves and reach a state of "relaxed concentration." Using relaxation skills can improve your state of mind, both on and off the playing field if you take the proper time to learn and hone these skills.

Chapter 10
The Art of Imagery

"He never blundered into victory, but won his battles in his head before he won them on the field."
Ralph Waldo Emerson

Before the 1976 Summer Olympics, the Soviet Union took pictures of the facilities in Montreal, studied them and pictured themselves competing there. So when they arrived, they had the feeling that they had been there before. American athletes are just beginning to realize the impact and importance of the mind-body connection in athletics while the European athletes have been utilizing and honing these skills for years.

One of the most powerful tools an athlete can use is that of imagery. The body cannot distinguish between something that is really happening, and something that they are visualizing. Take, for example, a bad dream, which I'm sure you've all had at one time or another. You wake up sweating, agitated and your heart pounding. Your body was physiologically reacting to something that had only occurred in your mind. Another example is if you were to remember an embarrassing event that happened to you. While recalling it you might start to blush or sweat – whatever it is you actually did in that particular situation, even though you are not physically encountering the event.

You've heard it called mental rehearsal, imagery, mental imaging and visualization – they all come from the premise of creating an experience in your mind. You create your own internal comfort zone. This chapter will address what imagery is and how you can best utilize it to improve your performance in all of your endeavors. Since the mind leads the body, this is an invaluable tool if it is done correctly and on a consistent basis. While playing for the Minnesota Vikings, Amad Rashad said that his imagination was a key to his success, "I got ready for a game by imagining every possible move a defender might use ... My imagination is stronger now than when I was growing up" (Dorfman & Kuehl, p. 143).

What is imagery

"Imagery is an art and a science. You get what you envision, not what you intend." Olympian Marilyn King

Imagery is a skill, a cognitive process in which you use your mind to create an experience that is not unlike the physical event. Mental rehearsal equals disciplined imagination. The goal is to use your mind to work on all aspects of your performance. For example, recalling the best day you ever had, error correction and putting yourself in different situations under all sorts of conditions to help take away the element of surprise are all ways to utilize this skill. To be effective, you need to practice imagery on a regular basis, just like physical performance. Your commitment to both must be equal.

Quality imagery is a way of programming your mind and body to perform more closely to perfection on a consistent basis (Orlick, 1990). Every person has the ability to visualize success, it's just a matter of doing it. Imagery provides the strength, energy and motivation for upcoming events by recalling, step-by-step, the feelings of success. The purpose of imagery is to achieve in your mind exactly what it is you want your body to do.

There are a couple of different theories on how imagery works. The first one is the Psychoneuromuscular Theory, which states that vividly imagined events produce an innervation in your muscles that is similar to that produced by physically executing the movement. The same neuromuscular units involved in the actual physical practice are occurring here as well, just in a slighter degree. Your brain is incapable of distinguishing between something that is actually happening and something that is vividly imagined. It works through facilitation of the neural pathway (Weinberg). This creates "muscle memory." Thus, imagery puts your mind through a neural workout that is not unlike the real thing.

Another theory is the Symbolic Learning Theory. This theory states that the rehearsal of a sequence of movements involved in a task is useful because movements are symbolic components of the task (Ungerleider & Golding). You are programming your muscles and preparing your body by forming a mental blueprint. This helps you create and code movement patterns that become more familiar to you the more you practice them.

You can visualize from either an internal or external perspective. If you are an internal watcher you are more kinesthetically oriented. From a physiological aspect this is most beneficial, and you more than likely learn best by trial and error. For the most part, it is best to try and be the person actually going through the motions so that you have a keen awareness of how it feels to do things the correct way. If you are an external watcher, you are more visually oriented and you probably learn best by watching others or videos. External imagery is good for error correction, this way you can see what it is you are actually doing wrong, as would your coach.

Believe it or not, imagery helps as much as physical practice. The more you practice executing your skills in your head, the more it becomes a conditioned response, second nature. Which is exactly what we want our skills to be – instinctive. As mentioned previously, this is a characteristic of peak performance. This also increases reaction time because there is no thought process, just action. We want our performances to seem effortless and flow. I'm sure you are familiar with Pavlov's experiment with dogs, well Alexander Romen of Russia took it one step further. He included not just physiological responses (salivation) but mental response conditioning. He showed that muscles actually performed the physical activity imagined or suggested by words, showing that psychoneurological factors that produce specific muscular responses can be programmed in advance through mental imagery (Garfield).

Lloyd Percival (1952) did a basketball study for four weeks with collegiate athletes. Group 1 did 20 minutes of predetermined shots. Group 2 did 5 minutes with eyes open, 10 minutes with eyes shut, then 5 more minutes with eyes open. Group 1 finished at 23/50, and Group 2 at 39/50. Group 2 did significantly better, and only had one-half of the actual practice time as Group 1. This sort of practice strengthens muscle memory, builds confidence and forces you to focus on sensations (Tutko & Tosi). This study reinforces how imagery is just as productive as physical training.

Just as with physical training, mental training should be done habitually. It should become a regular part of your practice schedule. You need to make the commitment and take the time to utilize this skill. Making excuses will not help you improve. You need to realize that there will always be other things you need to get done, or a seemingly better time to do this, but creating a conducive environment is an internal one – it's your choice to make this a priority or not. Practice is always in season, your mind is your practice field any day, any time, any place – it is always accessible.

The more on-site imagery you do in normal practice environments, the better off you are. After being in a car accident Olympian Marilyn King wasn't able to do any actual "physical" training so she had to do mental rehearsal – "I watched films and stood out on the track for hundreds of hours, envisioning in multi-sensory (technicolor), all of my events. It was an eye-opener to place second at the Olympic Trials with no physical training. It was life-altering for me." Imagery increases your ability to concentrate and stay focused. The ultimate objective is to experience the image with all your senses and end up centered on the activity, controlled and successfully obtaining your goals. If you can see yourself being successful you create an inner state of calm confidence and relaxation that attributes to success (Huang & Lynch).

Imagery exercises

In applying these techniques you must first achieve a deep relaxed state. Imagery is an extension of the relaxation process (follow the guidelines from the previous chapter). Go off by yourself, get comfortable, concentrate on your breathing and get your body relaxed. Start out easy and non-detailed by visualizing a simple scene and slowly add each of the senses (sight, taste, sound, smell, feeling). Then begin to introduce objects and situations relative to your sport. You are trying to create real, moving mental images. Become aware of which sense is most dominant for you – "feel," "I see," "I hear," etc.

While doing this you also need to rehearse the cues that accompany performance. You need to be aware of all your senses, especially kinesthetic cues, or body feeling. This helps you to recognize the important cues in competitive situations. It also helps you to make a discriminative cue analysis of various situations. Gaining control over your emotions and blocking out crowd noise can also be handled appropriately. You need to focus on, and be aware of, every aspect of the event.

We are going to go over a couple of non-sports related exercises to help you sharpen your imagery skills. The first one is a lemon exercise, it is an exercise in honing all of your senses as well as showing the power of the mind-body connection.

Exercise #8

Close your eyes and imagine that you have a lemon in your hand. Pick it up and feel the texture of it, see its bright yellow color, put it up to your nose and smell it. Once you have done that I want you to take a knife, cut the lemon in half and take a big bite of the lemon, ... (pause) and then another bite. What you should experience are two things. The first is that there is probably one sense that is most dominant and one that is difficult to imagine. For example, it may have been very easy to see the color of it, but you may have not been able to smell it. The second thing is that when you took a bite your mouth might have watered while you were "chewing and swallowing" the lemon, or your jaw may have tightened. We all know you were not really eating a lemon. But, your body was physiologically reacting to how you know (from past experience) a lemon tastes. It is very bitter and many times your mouth waters. This exercise shows how your body was reacting to something that was only happening in your mind (Adapted from Curtis, J., The Mindset for Winning, 1989, Coulee Press, Madison, WI).

Exercise #9

This next one is an exercise in being in control of your images. I want you to imagine your automobile. Imagine you are standing next to it, picture everything about it, and be as detailed as possible. Then, I want you to imagine that someone is slowly driving away from you down the street. See it in your mind getting smaller and smaller until you can't see it anymore. Once you are able to do that, I want you to imagine that your car is now being driven back towards you, imagine it getting bigger and bigger until it is parked next to you again. This is important because you need to have 100% control over your imagery. You are in control and calling all the shots in your mind.

Exercise #10

The last non-sports imagery requires a partner. In this imagery you need to be aware of only the relevant cues from the external environment. While you stand with your arms extended out at your side and your eyes closed, your partner will tell you that you have a bag in each hand. He will then tell you that there are different objects being put in each bag, 3 pounds in the left, 3 pounds in the right, etc. He will then make the weight distribution extremely uneven (i.e., 30 pounds in the left and 10 pounds in the right). You will then be asked to open your eyes without moving your arms. You will most likely find that one arm is much lower (weighed down) than the other due to the imagery exercise (Martens). Again, showing you how your body reacts to something that is created in your mind.

Once you have honed the skills by way of non-sport specific experiences you can then apply them in many different ways to help enhance your athletic performance.

We will address a few here:

1. The most common one is your peak performance. This is the one you would like to repeat over and over again. The performance was perfect, positive and you achieved your goal. The effectiveness of your imagery is enhanced when you have clear and concise goals. The success mechanism in your body is activated by goals. Goals provide direction and in turn help direct your images and mental rehearsal towards success. You should always keep in mind the selected goals and behaviors you hope to achieve.

   Go over the way you felt before, during and after the game. Visualize the experience in detail, using as many senses as possible, and be aware of the people, location, surroundings, etc. Visualize it from inside your body and feel each and every movement and all of the accompanying emotions. Carry it through to completion using the actual speed. For example, if it was a particular drive of a football game, and it took four minutes, then your imagery exercise should also be as close to four minutes as possible. If you are pitching or at the free throw line you control the tempo, so go at a pace that is comfortable for you.
2. Imagery allows you to put yourself in any situation imaginable so you can work on strategies and techniques that are most helpful in a given situation. Simulate game situations with scores already in place, see yourself coming from behind to win, maintaining a big lead, tying up the game, etc. Imagery is a buffered kind of learning that feels authentic in your mind yet lacks the consequences of the real world (Orlick). It allows you to enter scenes that you can never fully replicate in normal practice conditions. It is as effective and beneficial as the actual physical training itself. The stronger and more detailed the

image, the better your body can understand what it has to do, and the better the transfer of learning. Astronauts and pilots do this sort of simulation training (lack of gravity, take-off, etc.) so they can learn without the consequences of the real thing. For example, mentally as well as physically, putting you and your teammates through a 2-minute offensive drill in football can help mentally prepare you to be more calm, collected and productive in that highly stressful situation.

Imagery allows you to enter events with a feeling of having been there before – a sort of deja vu effect. You can then respond more effectively to expected, or unexpected, situations. “If one will attempt the most difficult endeavor his mind can possibly conceive and is successful in that venture, then everything else will seem easy by comparison,” said Nietzsche. You can get the "feel" of the desired performance by imagery. This way you can practice future events and prepare yourself as a **complete** athlete. You can furnish yourself with the proper tools necessary to deal appropriately with whatever is handed to you. “It is wise to consider all potentials of battle and negotiations before entering them. Rehearse them in your mind. Think of the consequences that may result from your actions. This will allow you to be better prepared ...” (Roberts p. 89).

You can also add shadowing to this experience, which is going through the actual physical motions to get the feeling of doing it correctly. This reinforces the correct skill movement (Tutko & Tosi). This way your body **and** your mind are getting the experience. For example, you would swing the bat imagining yourself hitting, the only thing missing from the actual experience would be the ball. A basketball player would stand at the free throw line (without the ball) imagining, and "physically" dribbling the ball a couple time and then shooting the basket.

3. Imagery can also be very helpful for error correction. If you come across a problem area, imagery allows you to slow things down and explore the problem. When you have difficulty in executing something, stop, relax, take a deep breath and then see yourself overcoming the difficulty and handling the situation successfully. You can then overlearn the preferred behavior to make the desired reactions automatic. This is a situation where it might be quite beneficial to view yourself from the outside so you can see what you are mechanically doing wrong. Then move to visualizing from an internal perspective once you have pinpointed the problem so that you can feel yourself doing it the correct way. One way to help with this is to mentally color code your body parts so you can isolate the area you need to be focusing on (Syer & Connolly). Since you have full control of the situation, you can also use this to help break bad habits.
4. There is also present moment rehearsal which is done during the actual competition. Though it has to be done relatively quickly just prior to the actual skill performance. This can be more effective is some sports than in others. For example, this could be used with great success by a pitcher as part of his pre-pitch routine, a hitter as part of his at-bat ritual, a basketball player about to shoot from the free throw line, or a kicker about to kick a field goal.
5. Using imagery for stressful or anxiety-provoking situations helps desensitize you to the emotions. By creating it over and over again in your mind, you will slowly be able to do it without the emotions and

anxiety that would usually handicap you. Your ability to handle these situations will improve with time and practice. For example, if you were hit in the head by a pitch, you may be fearful and tentative about going back to bat. Imagery could help you get over this fear by repetition and by recalling all the past positive experiences you have had before you got hit. Your fear will slowly be reduced.

6. Imagery can also be used to enhance your self-image. **We are what we think**. Your self-image is determined by the thoughts and images you hold in your mind, both consciously and unconsciously. Positive imagery can serve as a true confidence builder. Having a positive attitude about yourself is a key to success.

Two times to exercise this skill are before practice or competition and before you go to sleep. Before practice or a competition, just take a few minutes and picture what it is you want to achieve while you are out there. Don't just go through the motions – be thorough and use all of your senses. Picture yourself doing it perfectly. This will help increase your self-confidence and keep you motivated to reach your goals.

It's effective if you mentally rehearse every night before going to sleep. It is said that visualizing at that time is most beneficial because of the slow brain wave frequencies – you are in a dream-like state. You are sending messages through the nervous system to the appropriate muscles, which is said to accelerate the learning process. Just as studying before you go to sleep is said to be most effective because you will retain the most information. This is when you are the most relaxed and can open your mind and really concentrate. So, at night, find a comfortable, quiet place and picture yourself going through your routine or game. If you make a mistake, go back and correct it before continuing. Here's an interesting fact – one week after the 1984 Olympics, Mary Decker was interviewed regarding her fall in the 3000 meter race. She said she dreamed and visualized about the race, but never saw herself finish it (Porter & Foster, 1986).

Benefits and potential problem areas

There are many benefits of utilizing imagery skills, here we will name a few:

- ➡ Improves concentration
- ➡ Helps with error correction
- ➡ Aides in consistency
- ➡ Helps maintain skills while injured
- ➡ Enriches self-confidence
- ➡ Increases motivation
- ➡ Assists in your ability to control emotional responses
- ➡ You can practice your strategy
- ➡ Helps to cope with injury/pain
- ➡ Accelerates reaction time
- ➡ Improves physical coordination
- ➡ Assists in evaluating performances and pinpointing areas for further improvement
- ➡ Helps you to refocus if, for example, you have a bad pre-competition warm-up

Doesn't it seem beneficial, then, to use this skill to help enhance your athletic performance? As an athlete, it would seem that you would want **every** possible edge you can get! Isn't that right?

The possible barriers, or negative aspects, in relation to this technique are quite limited:

1. Just as positive imagery shapes your actions, so can negative imagery. If you mentally rehearse a failed action you will reinforce the wrong actions and all the negative feelings that accompany it. Anxiety, low self-esteem, fear of failure, a poor attitude and bad habits can all become part of what you carry into your game if you make them a part of your mental images.
2. You also need to make sure you carry your imagery through to completion, so you can increase your mental stamina and improve your concentration. Many times you "decide" you want to start over – with the attitude that it's just a practice, no harm done. In a real competition you don't have that choice, so your imagery and practice shouldn't be any different. You should practice toughing it out and dealing with the adversity, instead of wanting to give up and start over.
3. Focusing on the wrong cues for particular situations can be another barrier to successful imagery. It's the same as having bad (physical) practice habits. If you continue visualizing negative, destructive patterns and seeing undesirable results, you will imprint them into your mind. That is why it is important to know the appropriate cues for your sport.

You can't achieve something unless you can first see it in your mind's eye. Once you believe you can do it, then visualize yourself achieving it. You will have a much better chance of reaching your goals. Olympic Swimmer Amanda Beard has this to say about her ability to swim on instinct and focus, "I try to picture the whole race... I concentrate on all my muscles and breathing and heart rate. Then I visualize myself winning" (McNichol, p. 5).

Helping to turn your aspirations and desires into their physical equivalent is the goal of this technique. Ralston High School Baseball Coach, Curt Shockey, sums it up nicely, "Mental preparation is the ability to see yourself being successful. It's a process in which the body completes what the mind begins" (Brennan, p. 219).

Imagery is a skill that calls for precision and discipline. It puts you to work on setting correct moves and strategies firmly into your athletic routine. You can then see yourself as a winner and picture yourself doing the things that make you a winner. You are not just concentrating on the end results, but the means to the end. You guide your mind and are in complete control. It is the step-by-step thinking, practicing and doing that will help get you where you want to go. Your mental rehearsal should complement your physical training and can aid in learning new skills. The answer lies in your ability to channel your emotions and control your own game through imagery. This technique is a tool that allows you to take what you would most **like** to do and turn it into what you will most **likely** do.

"If you can imagine it you can achieve it. If you can dream it you can become it." William Arthur Ward

Chapter 11
Just Concentrate!

"Just concentrate!" That is one of the most frequently heard statements in sports. It sounds so simple, yet it can be very difficult to do at times – and many athletes are confused about "how" to concentrate. This chapter will address what concentration is, why concentration is broken, how to increase your ability to focus on the task at hand, and how to regain your focus and deal with distractions. I think we can all agree that a slight lapse in concentration can be very costly. Distractions are a big part of sport and life, so everyone needs to learn how to best deal with them so that performance is not diminished. A loss of focus will usually result in lost opportunities, more errors, and opponents taking advantage of your lack of focus. If you're not focusing 100%, you are not performing at your highest potential. If your thinking is not totally on the task at hand, your performance will not be up to par, even if it is just a slight lapse in concentration.

What is concentration?

Concentration is the ability to direct your senses and thought processes to particular objects, thoughts and feelings that are pertinent to the task at hand. Concentration can be equated with mental discipline and mental control. When you have a strong, controlled focus it can cut right through anything that seems to be standing in your way of achieving your goals. You can gain this control through awareness of your **body** and your **thoughts**; and then acting accordingly with your self-talk and physical behavior. Focusing is the narrowing of one's attention to a specific task and can vary in intensity and duration (i.e., pitchers vs. outfielders). Nideffer (1976) breaks it down this way – direction (external vs. internal) and width (broad vs. narrow). The ability to shift back and forth without interrupting the flow your play is important.

1. Broad/External – You are assessing the external situation (i.e., where the defenders are, who is on base, where the opportunities are, etc.).
2. Broad/Internal – After you organize the information, you need to devise a plan/strategy for yourself (i.e., a quarterback may find the open receiver and then decide the best way to get the ball to him; or if the baseball is hit your way – where is the play?).
3. Narrow/External – You need to react to specific environmental cues. For example, a hitter in baseball and softball needs to react to the pitcher's movement and release.
4. Narrow/Internal – It is then necessary to focus on your own internal body cues (self-talk, body tension, movement, etc.). From there you then focus on what action you should be taking.

Everyone **can** concentrate, it's just a matter of where you put your focus. "Can't concentrate" doesn't exist. People tend to concentrate and focus on things that are of direct interest to them. For example, if you are walking along the street and you hear someone mention your name, or your school's name, it will most likely grab your "attention." Also, things in motion will grab your attention. Babies, for example, are intrigued, and their attention captured, by things that move.

Why is concentration broken?

- ✔ Breaks in thought pattern because of distractions (external by way of other people, internal by way of your own invading thoughts of failure or thoughts of the future) can disrupt your concentration. Something becomes a distraction only when you let it. It is your choice to attend to, and acknowledge, it. Your physical skills don't disappear because of distractions, you let yourself lose the focus that allows you to perform effectively and successfully (Orlick).
- ✔ Attending to too many cues – Trying to do too many things at once leads to a divided focus. You lose the quality – you're doing two or more things subpar, instead of doing one thing well. It's better to be strong and focused in one area, than weak in every area. It is the specialist, as opposed to the generalist, who has the power (Ries, 1996).
- ✔ Lack of motivation – You view the task as unimportant so your attention wanders to things you deem as more interesting or important. If you have the incentive, are motivated in the right direction and are focused, then you can do great things.
- ✔ You are stressed, not relaxed, have no confidence or are too emotional. You need to have a clear mind and be focusing only on what is necessary. Don't clutter your mind with superfluous thoughts and feelings. Yogi Berra puts it quite succinctly, "A full mind is an empty bat."

Ways to improve concentration

1. Stay in the present moment and keep positive no matter what happens – You have to be able to stay on one even level. Your attitude and desire to do this

plays a big part in your success. "You take it kick by kick, you don't look to the future, you don't look to the past. If you missed that last kick, you've got to forget about it and go out there and get the next one," says former San Francisco 49er Kicker Jeff Wilkins. Live the moment, seize the day, carpe diem!

2. Have a single-minded focus – "Just like a company, each person has their own job. I focus only on one person. A corner can't think about stopping the run (unless he sees it), if he does that's a breakdown mentally. I concentrate only on my coverage. I don't hear anything when I'm out there. After the play I regroup. I don't think about whether I did good or bad, I just move on," says San Francisco 49er Marquez Pope. You must have one mind set and total concentration to get the most out of your abilities.
3. Have a 1-pointed intention – Hold your attention to the intended outcome with such unbending purpose that you absolutely refuse to allow obstacles to consume and dissipate the quality of your attention. Your intention is for the future, but your attention must be in the present for you to have the future you desire. Focus on the process, not the results, paradoxically, your nonconcern for the results will help you perform even better and get the results you desire.
4. Concentrate on what you need to do, not what to avoid – Don't wander to past errors or the future (stay in the present). When you try to "not" do something, that very thing you are trying to avoid usually becomes your dominant focus. "Don't look over there" is a perfect example. If someone says that to you, where does your focus go? It goes to the exact place you were told not to look! Trying too hard results in you not accomplishing what you want, and makes you "press" under pressure.

5. Know the attentional demands of your sport – This includes the relevant cues necessary to perform well such as, "What should I concentrate on in a specific situation?" and "When should I be attending to what?" "When should my attention be broad or narrow and internal or external?" Write all of this down so that you have a clear understanding of what your job is.
6. "Grant me the serenity to accept the things I cannot change, the courage to change the things I can, and the wisdom to know the difference." Reinhold Neibuhr Focusing on things you can control is of utmost importance. You can't control situations and obstacles, but you can control your emotions, reactions and thoughts. You need to realize that there are many things that are going to be out of your control. Things may happen that seem unfair, but you have to make the best of it and focus on things within your control. To focus on the other things is a waste of time and energy and will just leave you frustrated. You can only control your level of play. You need to be able to rationally assess the situation, and then identify and exercise appropriate and effective responses.
7. Your breathing (count breaths) "In, one"; "Out, two," can help improve your focusing ability. Don't pass judgement on yourself if you lose your focus or are distracted. Accept it for what it is, a lapse in concentration, and then get back to the task ("I was on breath number 4..."). Relaxation is an exercise in maintaining and strengthening focus and aids in your ability to control anxiety. It helps you focus on the task at hand by bringing your attention to one thing, your breathing – the present. You are trying to get yourself "centered." Which is the process by which we move from the busy periphery of our lives inward to a silent place. Direct your thoughts internally to

mentally check in. It's a way to gain control and focus on one spot – your center (behind your belly button).

8. Cues help create the appropriate association and serve as triggers to the proper action. To help you better understand cues and how they work here's an example. Think about your favorite CD, the one you play over and over again and know by heart. Now, if you were in your car and you heard the first song from that favorite CD, what would you **automatically** do when that song was over? You would, most likely, expect song 2 to start. You'd have to take a minute and realize that it is on the radio, not your CD. The end of the first song served as a **cue** or trigger for the second song. If a certain action (tapping your heel with your bat) or a word (relax) is used often enough it will serve as a **cue** to the desired response.
9. Imagery – Put yourself in certain situations and focus on success. Be sure to use all your senses. This will increase your confidence and help you feel in control and prepared. Simulate different situations (noise, consequences) so that you can practice keeping your focus and regaining it if you find yourself distracted.
10. Chevreul's Pendulum – Take a piece a string and attach a weight (nut, bolt, etc.) to the bottom. Hang it in front on you and focus on it (you may want to put your elbow on a table to help steady your hand). Keep your hand still. Mentally see it moving in a circle, the actual action will follow (be patient, it takes practice). Once you get really good at it you can make it go one way, stop it and make it go the other way. What is happening is you are sending nerve impulses to your hand to make it move and since the impulses are ever so slight, the string and bolt are just exaggerating the impulses. (Adapted from Curtis, J., The Mindset for Winning, 1989, Coulee Press, Madison, WI)

11. Concentration grid – On a grid of 100, if you get in the upper 20's that equals great concentration. But don't be discouraged if you get less then ten the first few times, just like everything else, it takes practice. To do this exercise you will need a timer that is set for one minute. Once you start the timer find 01 on the grid and put a slash through it and continue sequentially until the timer stops. As you become more familiar with the grid, you can start backwards from 100, make a new grid, or introduce distractions (radio, TV) so that you are constantly challenging yourself. The goal is to be able to stay focused on this task without being distracted or having your mind wander to other things.

04	40	13	83	45	20	03	27	35	09
54	98	69	30	52	86	49	94	63	47
68	74	90	19	79	58	25	56	24	91
84	59	66	53	95	34	44	88	16	73
29	22	31	80	26	07	62	51	46	08
11	70	76	41	10	36	92	18	71	81
60	67	100	14	87	82	15	28	33	57
39	05	55	77	37	23	65	43	99	17
97	75	01	61	48	42	96	02	72	78
32	89	12	21	93	06	38	50	64	85

12. Watch videos – What **should** you be attending to? What **are** you attending to? Are there any discrepancies?
13. Simon – The children's game "Simon" is a good exercise in honing concentration skills. One slight lapse in concentration and you "lose."

14. Take an object, focus in on it and say “ball” or “glove” (identifying the object) and then line up objects and practice shifting your focus. Or, take a sentence and focus on the whole sentence, then focus in tightly on one word, then the whole page. Practice changing your focus from broad to narrow without losing your concentration. Then do it with distractions (radio, people talking in a busy room, etc.).
15. Then apply it to your sport. For example, narrow your focus going from viewing the whole pitcher to the logo on his cap, then to a spot on the ball after his release. Or, focus on the seams of the ball to keep your focus narrow and in the here-and-now. Then, watch the ball all the way to the plate, don’t squint – relax. Being tight will negatively effect your vision.
16. You need to know under what circumstances your attention wanders. Awareness is the key. A good way to gain this understanding is to keep a journal. In this record any time when your concentration was broken or you couldn’t regain your focus and describe how you were distracted (externally or internally, and by what?). It’s important to identify your obstacles. The quicker you can identify your distractions, the quicker you can let them go. Write down the things that you are most commonly distracted by. Many times you will learn something that you didn’t know, or didn’t notice, until you saw it on paper. You can also learn how a certain pattern developed by keeping a journal. Always be aware of your surroundings.

At practice don’t just focus your attention on the things you do well, focus training on your weaker links also. This is why evaluating your play is so important, so that you know what things need extra focus and attention. The athletes that succeed are the ones that focus on all aspects of the game. Sports Attorney Rockne Lucia, Jr., on Oakland A's Pitcher Tom Candiotti, "Tom is a very focused guy. He has basically worked towards this goal for all his life... He's a smart player. He knows how to train, he uses his mind and his body."

Learn to break things down into more manageable units. For example, if you have to run 100 laps, focus on running 1 lap 100 times, this way your focus is always on the present. Focusing on 100 laps at once will make the task much harder. Or, instead of thinking of practice as a long and grueling 3 hours. View it as 15 minutes of stretching, 20 minutes for this drill, 15 minutes for that drill, etc.

You also need to lead up to each game the same way. Be consistent in terms of your approach, arousal level and confidence at the start of each competition. From warm-up to game don't change anything. It's called "warm-up" for a reason. You shouldn't practice one thing and then do another, there is no logic or consistency in that. Your pregame warm-up is to help narrow your focus, get your body ready and get in the groove, so that you can react instinctually in the game. Focus only on game-relevant things, remove all other distractions. If you do experience a setback, don't panic. Let it serve as a reminder to focus only on performance cues and to redirect energy to things within your control.

What if your concentration is broken?

If your concentration is broken, or you have trouble regaining focus after a mistake, there are a few ways to deal with this:

1. Rituals – Rituals help to calm you down and focus on the task at hand. They provide consistency to your approach, which intensifies your focus and increases

your confidence. You can have pre-game rituals as well as rituals you use during a game or competition. Rituals and routines give you a sense of control and stability in an unstable environment. Get pre-performance ritual/routine down before the season starts so that you are comfortable with it and not still experimenting when the season gets under way. Many athletes use changing into their uniform as a trigger to get ready to go play.

Don't confuse rituals with superstitions. Superstitions are different in that you base performance on things that aren't always in your control, and are built on irrational associations. Superstitions can be a kind of negative self-fulfilling prophecy. For example, if you say you have to eat a certain food before you play, and that food is not available, you then convince yourself that you aren't going to play well. And, in turn, you don't! Many athletes also feel superstitious that if their ritual is not carried out to completion they won't be able to perform well. More times than not, this is just an excuse for a bad performance ("I didn't have time to go through my pre-game properly – that's why I didn't play well!"). Good luck is nothing more that preparation meeting opportunity (Chopra). You create your own luck.

2. Focal points – These are reminders of what your intention is, and how hard you've worked up to this point. It also serves as a release to get rid of anything unproductive in your head. Pick a stable point on your field/court and have that be the place you go to when you lose your focus or are distracted. Focus in on that one thing (2nd base, field goal posts, upper corner of volleyball net, etc.), and take a deep breath so you can

regain your composure and put your focus back on one thing – yourself. This will help bring you back to the present and the task at hand. Note that the examples I've mentioned are all things that are very specific and will be at all games no matter where you play. If you were to pick a specific sign on your outfield wall, what would you do at away games? This is why it is necessary to pick something that will always be there, no matter where you are playing.

3. Other releases – Pick up some dirt and then "throw away" negative emotions. Or, go over to your bag and put your negative emotions in it and "zip it up" – you can address it later. You can be creative here, find something that works well for you.
4. Use your circle breathing to put your focus back on yourself and back in the present moment. Your mind and body have to be in the same time – the present (offense vs. defense, hitting vs. playing infield). Your mind can't be back in the 1st quarter if your are physically in the 3rd.

"Hold your thoughts to the present ... Actions that spring from this attitude will be appropriate." I Ching no. 52

You need to be absorbed in the moment and forget about everything else and focus only on yourself. The best and the elite competitors forget who they are competing against, they forget about the crowd; they are just immersed in the moment – the fun, the challenge, the task at hand. Who you are playing against, where you are playing, rankings – all those things shouldn't change your focus. You focus only on yourself and your teammates. "Once there is a group of 11, everything outside of that is shut out," says San Francisco 49er Wide Receiver J.J. Stokes.

Focus on your own task, what you need to do. What your particular task is should be your only concern. Anything else will cause you to falter. If you do this it will increase your confidence and make you feel in control and prepared. The key is to focus on your own game, not other people's. If everyone concentrated on what they needed to do, the team as a whole would be much better off.

"Don't complain about the snow on your neighbor's roof when your own doorstep is unclean." Confucius

This chapter has educated you on what concentration is, why it is broken, and given many ways to help you improve your ability to concentrate, as well as ways to regain your focus when necessary. **You need to focus your talent, time and energy on getting things done that need to be done RIGHT NOW**. Staying in the present and focused on the task at hand cannot be stressed enough. It is the key to keeping your focus and regaining your focus.

"... he does not live in the present, but with reverted eye laments the past, or, headless of the riches that surround him, stands on tiptoe to foresee the future." Ralph Waldo Emerson

Chapter 12
Positive Self-talk

"It's not what you think you are that holds you back, it's what you think you are not."

Take a minute and think about all the dialogue that goes on in your head while you are playing. Does this thinking help you perform efficiently and productively? Does this thinking give you added confidence? Is this thinking in your own best interest? I think you'll be very surprised at the answers. People may or may not be products of their environment, but they are products of their thoughts (Bennett & Pravitz, 1982). What you think becomes your reality. "Nothing has any power over me other than that which I give it through my conscious thought" (Robbins, 1986, p. 88).

Many times, you don't need a competitor or opposing team to beat you. You can do that all on your own by saying negative things to yourself while you are performing or playing a game. You can either be your own best friend or your own worst enemy – the choice is yours. It is very basic - positive self-talk will help your performance, negative self-talk will worsen it. Positive self-talk helps you to develop secure attitudes toward your performance and validates your capabilities. Self-defeating thoughts full of emotion just perpetuate your fears and doubts. Fear, anxiety and doubt are destructive to your mental well-being. Negative self-talk is just setting yourself up for misery. You need to learn to control your emotions or they will control you.

Positive Affirmation Statements

Positive affirmation statements are short statements designed to enhance self-image, help you achieve a secure mental attitude and increase confidence. Take, for example, Muhammed Ali's affirmation "I am the greatest." Other examples are:

"I live for the present."
"I am relaxed."
"I believe in my abilities."

Effective affirmations are clear, realistic, personal, believable and in the present tense. They will also aid you in achieving your goals. Changing your self-talk is going to play an enormous role in increasing your chance for successful performances on a more consistent basis. William Shakespeare said, "Nothing is good or bad, but thinking makes it so." The all important first step in this process is **monitoring your own thoughts**; the next step is **controlling them**. If you're able to control your thoughts, you can accomplish more than you were aware of – the task is a hard one, but more than worth the effort. It's important to use repetition with your affirmation statements. This will help embed them in your head. Now, let's get started:

1. You first need to identify situations in which you tend to be negative. For every negative thought come up with two positive ones to replace the existing negative self-talk (see Table 2). Every time you find yourself saying something negative, stop right there and turn

it around to something positive and constructive – this is called thought stopping. For example, "I hope I don't choke again today." becomes "I'm going to relax, trust my instincts, and I'll do great." Using lead-ins like "I am," "I will," and "I can" are very powerful and can effect your feelings and perceptions about a situation. Repeat these specific statements to yourself over and over.

Table 2

Negative statement	Positive statement
I'll never be able to do this	I'm going to put forth my best efforts and trust my instincts
We have no chance of beating them	I'll just concentrate on my task and my game
This drill is boring	This drill will help me be more consistent in games

You should make a similar table (or use this one) and put in the top ten negative things you say to yourself, and in the next column put a countering positive statement (or two) to replace the old one.

2. While practicing or competing, use cue words that describe, direct, are in the present tense and activate performance; i.e, "Keep my head up," or "Follow through." These cue words can help you move from thinking to reacting. Rehearse these new patterns. Write out specific statements and read them to yourself, and really believe what you are saying, otherwise doubts will persist. One of the most common things people say is, "I can't." That sort of statement needs to be changed to "I know I can do it;" "I've done it many times before;" "I will do it." You can also get energy from your positive statements, "I'm energized and ready to go." You want to keep your self-talk in accordance with the goals you have set for yourself.
3. Another thing that is helpful is keeping a journal. Write in it everyday after a practice or game while it is still fresh in your mind. Write down what your thoughts were before, during and after (both positive and negative). Then, go back and see where improvements can be made and make that a goal for the following day or next game. Also, by keeping a journal you might be able to see patterns or trends that you are inclined to fall into during certain situations; and from this, new and better patterns can be developed. A journal is also a form of letting go of things that are bothersome to you. By being able to put your feelings and thoughts down on paper you are able to move on a little more quickly and troubleshoot more efficiently.

If you say something enough times, you tend to act in ways which reflect this. That goes for both positive statements as well as negative. And, overattention to negative thoughts often leads to self-criticism. Self-talk can be destructive if you are labeling yourself as lazy, a failure, quitter, etc. You need to talk to yourself as you would speak to your best friend and back it up with the appropriate determination and action.

You can undermine your self-talk by:

1. Denial - This can negate the validity of a fine performance (by saying it was "just luck") or it can be an attempt to place blame elsewhere after a disappointment.
2. Rationalization – This is a more philosophical form of denial. You resign yourself to the idea that things simply happened that were beyond your control. And, nothing you could have done would have changed it, especially your internal dialogue!
3. Repression - Here you withhold your inner feelings about your performance and behavior from everyone, even from yourself. Although, you can only repress your feelings for so long until they surface one way or another.

These three things can negate a lot of the positive things you are saying to yourself. That's why it is important to take responsibility for the thoughts and actions that are within your direct control and deal with them accordingly.

Unless you take control of your own thoughts, they will control you and many things will be left to chance. That's why it is important to recognize thoughts and emotions that inhibit you and replace them with a winning attitude and constructive thoughts. W. Somerset Maugham said, "It's a funny thing about life, if you refuse to accept anything but the best, you very often get it" (Robbins, 1986, p. 38). Stay positive and don't settle for anything less than your best. You want this positive way of thinking to become habit (a behavior that is so well learned and practiced that is occurs almost automatically in certain situations), so that in the heat of competition, your mind will be your biggest fan, your best ally. The mental messages you tell yourself are directly correlated to the quality of the action about to be taken.

You can also use self-talk to aid in skill acquisition by giving yourself instructional cues (arm straight, head high, weight back). As the skills become well-learned cut down on the number of cues. Skills should become automatic and require only one or so cue words/phrases (i.e., smooth, follow-through) that are more general. The cues you say to yourself should reduce tension, not increase it. They should serve as a trigger to the appropriate action.

Believe wholeheartedly in the affirmations that you are telling yourself. The beliefs we hold were learned and can be unlearned if necessary. Believe what you say, even if it is not true at the moment – when you were "learning" all the limiting beliefs they were also not true (Porter & Foster). "The more positive you think, the more positive results you can expect. That has always been my philosophy and I live with that philosophy," says Bob Quinn, Ex-General Manager, NY Yankees, Cincinnati Reds, SF Giants.

"The one thing over which you have absolute control is your thoughts. It is this that puts you in a position to control your own destiny." Paul G. Thomas

Chapter 13
Improving Your Self-Confidence

"It's confidence, it's a function of confidence. Probably the biggest buzz word in sports is confidence – getting to where you want to go and then staying there."
Rockne Lucia, Jr., Sports Attorney

Successful athletes say a key to their success is not only believing in themselves, but also outwardly displaying self-confidence in their play. There seems to be a correlation between the two - success and self-confidence. When you think of the word confidence, many things come to mind: belief, faith, reliance, trust, poise, self-assurance, certainty, conviction and determination. All of these things are necessary for a team to play at a top level and be successful. If you don't believe in yourself, how do you expect your teammates and coaches to believe in you? "In the pros there are a lot of guys that can run fast, the talent level evens out. So how good **you think you are** is a motivating factor, and is what makes you better than the next guy," says former San Francisco 49er, Dr. Jamie Williams.

True self-confidence is an athlete's realistic expectation about achieving success. These expectations are a big part of who you are and what you will or will not achieve. It's a state of being, a feeling about who you are and what you are capable of achieving. Success has nothing to do with what you **hope** to do, but what you realistically **expect** to do. Athletes with optimal self-confidence set realistic goals they can achieve and that will perpetuate their success. Even then, you need to have the skills and work hard to back up your confidence. All the self-confidence in the world can't replace the physical tools and knowledge essential for sports. There must be confidence not only in yourself, but also in your teammates. For example, as a pitcher, your only concern should be pitching – once the ball is in play you have to trust that your defense will then do their job. Not having confidence in your teammates could lead to a division in your concentration and focus. Confidence in your teammates is great for the morale of the team and is a key to success. Great things will usually happen when a high level of confidence is present.

Performance will deteriorate when there is too much or too little confidence. But, regardless of whether there is too much or too little, the result is the same: lack of motivation and effort. The first because you feel it isn't necessary and you become complacent; the latter because you usually have the attitude of, "Why bother? – it won't do any good anyway." You want to be realistically confident, not under or over confident. You're not going to improve if you have your head in the clouds or by faking your true confidence level. Failing at critical moments can come from both under and over estimating your ability. Your attitude will be a factor in whether or not you succeed in what you have set out for yourself. A confident approach is an assertive approach with a high expectancy of success.

If you lack self-confidence and doubt yourself, you can fall into the trap of a negative self-fulfilling prophecy – meaning that the shear fact that you expect something negative to happen increases the chances of it actually becoming a reality. The expectancy of failure gives way to the behaviors that coincide with this thinking. You then begin to behave in accordance with those doubts, expecting failure and ultimately failing – thus confirming your original doubts and fears. In a way, you are apologizing in advance for your failure, this way your coach will not expect much from you. Another example is when you are typecast by either parents, coaches or teammates in a certain way (i.e., a goof-off, lazy), you tend to then act in agreement with this. Self-fulfilling prophecies that are perpetuated by a coach's negative impression of an athlete can effect the interaction between them.

Self Esteem

High self-esteem is present when there is little discrepancy between a person's ideal and actual self. This is a prerequisite for successful performance. It makes you more comfortable with yourself, your teammates, and your coaches. Unfortunately, two-thirds of the population suffer from low self-esteem. Realizing that you must live up to your own standards, not the standards of others, is very important.

Be aware that self-esteem, or lack of, is at the root of all behavior, both positive and negative and is made up of both your self-worth and self-trust. Self-worth is that you're glad you are who you are. Self-trust is the functional belief in your own ability to control what happens to you in a world of uncertainty. No opinion or judgement is so vitally important to your own growth and development as that which you hold of yourself. Remember, no one will ever critique you as sharply and critically as you. Your self-image is the external manifestation of your internal sense of self-esteem (opinion and evaluation of yourself with regards to your worth and competence). Having a positive self image gives you extra courage and **confidence** for all situations. A positive self-image is one of the most significant, and vulnerable, assets you can possess. (Syer & Connolly).

How to build and maintain confidence

"Confidence = concentration = control. If you don't have the first one, your concentration may wane and your control may not be there." Bob Quinn, Ex-General Manager, NY Yankees, Cincinnati Reds, SF Giants

1. Goal setting – Pick an area where slight improvement could occur quickly with little work and make this a goal. Know your strengths as well as your weaknesses, and view weaknesses as challenges to build on. Looking at your strengths will help give you the confidence to do this. Unfortunately, athletes tend to blur all parts of their game together and judge the whole by the weakest part. As a result, they tend to suffer from low self-confidence. But, by setting and achieving specific short-term goals, you gain confidence in yourself and your abilities as an athlete. It then becomes a positive cycle – success breeds confidence and confidence breeds success. It's a win-win situation. Goal setting gives you the structure necessary to have step-by-step success.
2. Positive self-talk – What you say to yourself during practice and game situations can have either a negative or positive effect on your confidence, and in turn, on the outcome. By sticking with positive affirmation statements, you keep yourself in a good mind set and can stay focused and confident on the task at hand. For example, "I am in control and ready

for success." Confidence is a state of mind you can intentionally evoke. By saying positive things to yourself, you can increase your confidence in your ability to perform the necessary tasks.

3. Body language – You must not only believe in the self-talk you are expressing, but also back it up with the proper body language; i.e., head held high, jog on and off the field/court, no emotion while at bat or shooting a free throw, etc. Don't give your opponent the psychological edge by looking defeated (head down, quiet). Carry yourself the same, and "act as if" you are doing great (confident, assured) and not at all phased by any turn of events. This "acting as if" lets you try on a different identity than the one you presently have. It's amazing, if you "act as if" negativity tends to bounce right off you. Use affirmations such as, "I'll receive what I believe." And, smile – it is said to take 72 muscles to frown and only 14 to smile. So conserve energy, no frowns! The changes that occur are the same whether you really feel that way or are "acting as if." Take for example, if you are in a bad mood and someone tells you a joke and you laugh, you perk up even though you don't want to, the effect is the same as if you were generally happy.

   Never show weakness or defeat on the outside. Opponents will try to psych you out more so by their outward behavior than by words. If you take it on an emotional level you will most likely be effected; therefore, you need to try and rise above it and play your own game. When your opponent is more focused on you than their own game take advantage! Don't play these ego games, play your own game.

4. Imagery – Recall past experiences where you were successful and build on them. Refer to them whenever

necessary, especially during times of self-doubt. Make the images as real as possible, put yourself back in the situation using as many senses as possible and stir up all the feelings that went along with this. Confidence increases when you see yourself succeed in difficult situations. ***Remember, past successes and past failures are real, but the failures you fear in the future are all in your mind.*** Fear is apprehension about the future and tells you "you can't."

One time when I was working with a figure skater, I asked this athlete to picture herself in a competition performing successfully. She came back the first few times saying she either saw herself falling on her most difficult items; or, if she was successful, it wasn't her face competing, it was that of her top competitor's! She didn't have enough confidence in her own abilities to be successful. It took a lot of repetition, but she was finally able to see **herself** skating a perfect program. Her confidence increased tremendously and her skating improved as a result.

5. Make a list of your positive attributes and past successes and keep them close by to look at. Don't be shy about praising your good qualities. Keep positive experiences in the forefront of your mind. Your own sense of value determines the quality of your performance.
6. Tape record yourself immediately after a successful experience so that you can refer back to it when necessary. Don't leave out a single detail!
7. Redefine success in terms of things that you have control over. Be process-oriented, not outcome-oriented. Don't define success in terms of win/loss record, but in the quality of your performance.
8. Chart performance and improvements and acknowledge when progress is made.

9. Be prepared – Thoroughly scout the other teams, this way you can be overly prepared and not be fearful of the competition. Don't let anyone catch you off guard, be as mentally and physically prepared as possible.
10. Take a compliment when given to you, don't dispute it because you lack confidence, use compliments to build your self-confidence. Confidence is improved through positive words by coaches, teammates and family.
11. Learn to trust your instincts – You need to have faith and trust your instincts. Trust that you have trained and prepared properly, so you will get the results you desire. We spoke about the importance of trusting your instincts and intuition as characteristics of peak performers in Chapter 1. "Every man discriminates between the voluntary acts of his mind and his involuntary perceptions, and knows that to his involuntary perceptions a perfect faith is due," said Ralph Waldo Emerson. Former San Francisco 49er Kicker Jeff Wilkins knows the importance of trusting his instincts and having confidence, "You have to have your mind straight in order to be able to go out there and kick that ball. You can have all the talent in the world, but if you're scared to death upstairs, or you don't have any confidence, you're not going to make that kick."

The most significant thing is for you to have confidence in your ability to acquire the proper mental and physical skills. With this kind of confidence, you will not be phased or intimidated by opponents or disturbed by temporary failures or setbacks. You will more likely view an isolated game/practice as a measure of your progress as you pursue your long-term goals. Play the game the way you know how – with talent, determination and the understanding of what needs to be done and how to do it. And, just by knowing that - you gain confidence. You need to have a high tolerance for adversity and setbacks to be able to be successful and persevere in athletics and life. Remember, problems are really opportunities to achieve something even greater. Failure and success are equal opportunities for learning. When you fail to learn, you have learned to fail. When Thomas Edison was attempting to make the lightbulb, he failed many times. Although in his eyes, he didn't fail, he just discovered another way not to do it!

High self-confidence gets you moving toward success instead of trying to avoid failure. If you do fail, which you will do from time to time, don't hang on to those failures. Babe Ruth struck out 1330 times, but he also had 714 homeruns. To be successful you need to deal with and master failure. You also need to admit and face your fears. When things are going wrong, your confidence decreases and you continually focus on what you are doing wrong, instead of how to get yourself out of the situation. The past failures that you are focusing on just increase the likelihood that you will experience more failure due to this thinking.

Evaluate your performance not yourself, your acts are measurable, you, as a total human being, are not. You will still be a valuable person regardless of your sporting results. This is a very basic fact, but one many people seem to forget. Before you were competing, you were a good, valuable person, and nothing can change that, not temporary failure or termination from your sport. Mistakes and lessons aren't direct judgements about you as a person, just feedback on how you can improve. You need to admit mistakes, don't make excuses, learn from them and then do your best not to repeat them. Ask yourself - "What's the worst case scenario?" This will help you deal with the fear and help put things in perspective. Fear usually makes your imagination run wild and conjure up things that will most likely **never** happen.

How your beliefs effect you

"Believe that your life is worth living and your belief will help create the fact." William James

People like there to be consistency with their thoughts, opinions and behaviors - this is just human nature. If you believe there is a discrepancy you will most likely want to make a change. People are uneasy if they believe one thing and then do another, so one will have to change so there is no discrepancy. People are very resistant to ideas that threaten their beliefs. Your beliefs are based on your environment, events, knowledge and past results. Your future is strongly affected by what you believe to be true. Beliefs are built on past experiences along with our perceptions of how things **should** be. Your beliefs have to be consistent with the results you desire.

As long as you are physically able, your performance will be strongly effected by your own beliefs and confidence in your abilities. This will also determine how much effort you put forth. If you have a strong belief, then no one can sway you. You are the greatest expert of you. All actions are a result of your beliefs and perceptions. "There can be a player with the natural ability to play at the major leagues but he remains at the minor leagues because, while all the physical tools and stats are there, he can't quite convince himself that he belongs. So much of it is believing you belong, but it has to be a sincere belief. It's tough to separate those," says Bob Quinn, Ex-General Manager, NY Yankees, Cincinnati Reds, SF Giants.

The greatest barriers in life are self-imposed. Limitations exist only in your mind. The 4-minute mile is a perfect example of this, once Roger Bannister did it in 1954, others followed suit (45 more in the next 18 months). It wasn't that their physical make-up changed, just their belief that it was possible. So it would seem that we all function far below are maximum mental and physical capability, until something triggers us. We've all heard amazing stories of someone lifting a car to save someone, or swimming great lengths to survival. When our back are to the wall and our lives are at stake, we can accomplish more than we ever thought possible. Although, you shouldn't have to be in a life-threatening situation to believe in yourself to accomplish something others thought you couldn't do. Be confident in your abilities, never believe the odds are against you. Blind yourself to the odds and realize actual competitions are not based on the odds, but on performance skills executed on that given day.

By shaking your opponents belief that they are going to be successful, their confidence is greatly effected. Many times teams do this by taking time-outs. Time-outs can be a form of momentum shifter. If one football team is driving effortlessly down the field, the other team will most likely take a time-out to kill the momentum of the other team and give them time to think about how well they are doing, which can lead to problems and effect their confidence.

Don't let other people's opinions effect your belief system. Don't give their opinion more weight than it deserves. Your confidence should come from within, you shouldn't let what others say have an effect on what you think of yourself. You also shouldn't let others opinion determine how confident you are. Although it seems that many times we let other people's opinions and beliefs effect us much more than they should. Many times coaches can have a negative effect on a player's self-confidence if they continually compare him to other members of the team, it will make him more tentative and self-conscious during practice or games. If, as a coach, you feel you need to make comparisons to get a point across, pick a player from another team that has the same qualities.

Stories of confidence

In the movie Rudy, Rudy's dad told him that, "not everyone is meant to go to college and that Notre Dame is for rich, good athletes not Rudingers." But fortunately, Rudy did not buy into his dad's belief system even though all his life people told him it couldn't be done. He said, "Someday I'm going to come out of that tunnel and run on to this field (Notre Dame football field)." He persevered – he was turned down three times before he was accepted to school there. He persisted, he made the team and got to play one play with one of the best college football teams. His ability was small, but his heart and persistence were huge – and his teammates loved him for it. Since 1975 no other player has been carried off the field.

"I had a moment where I went into a competition thinking I'm so-so, I work harder than anyone else, but I'm not that great. Then they invited someone I had beaten to the Olympic training camp and I knew I was a better athlete than she was. So my thinking, in a moment, went from I'm so-so to – they think she could be in the Olympics and I'm better than she is. That means I could be in the Olympics." 2-time Olympian Marilyn King

"I had supreme confidence – intergalactic confidence. I was able to convince myself I could save the day. I was Spiderman or Batman (dark knight on the field). I read comic books pre-game – part of the confidence thing. I did these things to help my mind escape and suspend my level of reality and believe that for that moment, those 4 quarters, that I was a superhero and I had things I had to save, had to save people, save my team. Whatever it took, I had to beat my man." Former San Francisco 49er, Dr. Jamie Williams

Confidence is something that is a must in everything you do. If you don't have it, you will always fall short of your objectives because you will most likely quit in the middle due to some setback or adversity instead of sticking it out. If you have true confidence in your abilities then you will persevere and keep striving for the goals you have set for yourself. What you believe yourself to be will effect everything you do. You've got to "be" before you can "do" and you've got to "do" before you can "have." You have to be able to trust your instincts and not second-guess yourself. You must have enough confidence to let your brain and nervous system take over without any interference from your conscious mind. Be confident that your body knows what to do based on all of your mental and physical preparation. Self-confidence is acquired, it isn't inherited. Even once you acquire it, you have to take measures to sustain it and it must constantly be attended to. You need to think and act like a champion.

"Human beings, by changing the inner beliefs of their minds, can change the outer aspects of their lives." American Philosopher William James

Chapter 14
Handling Adversity

In sports, and in life, things don't often go as planned and there are glitches that need to be dealt with. This final chapter will address three of the most common problems that athletes are faced with: choking, slumps and injury. Many of the skills that were addressed in this book can be used to not only help deal with these things, but can also be used in a preventative fashion.

Choking

Have you ever "choked" at a game? Left your skills on the practice field? Lost your focus after making an error or striking out? I'm sure every one of you can answer yes to at least one of these questions. If you play sports you have most likely choked at one time or another. Rod Laver said, "Maybe it won't be any consolation, but you ought to know, I've choked, still do sometimes ... And I've never met anybody who hasn't" (Tutko & Tosi, p. 25). I'm sure you can ask any athlete from high school to the pros and they'll say the same thing. No one is going to be perfect all of the time.

Coaches and athletes both pose the same question - why do players choke? And, how can it be avoided? The bigger question is how can a team stay relaxed, focused, and mentally tough from practice all the way to the competition - which is the antithesis to choking. We can't eliminate choking all together, but we can reduce the tendency for this to happen.

Choking stems from your need for psychological safety. The more threatening a competitive event is to your psychological safety, the more stressful and disruptive the situation will seem. Although, there are times when choking stems from poor preparation and lack of self-confidence. Some may try to make excuses, and attribute it to lack of effort in a particular situation or something external. Coaches may suffer from this from time to time as well. This happens when they are put in a situation that they perceive as important and don't have the ability to make good decisions, or they stray from the game plan when they shouldn't.

Choking starts out as a cognitive problem and ends up a physical one, and thus negatively effects performance. Choking begins with negative self-talk and fear. It is the interpretation of a task as threatening, or a situation as extremely important, which causes feelings of tension and anxiety, both of which distract you from the task at hand and therefore impede performance (Scott & Pelliccioni, 1982). The key word is interpretation, because in actuality, the situation isn't making you tense, you are making yourself tense. Believe it or not, anxiety doesn't exist outside of your own head. You start questioning your ability to get a hit, complete a pass, throw a strike, make a play, etc. All these negative thoughts begin snowballing and pretty soon you're thinking about consequences, your next shot – just a whirlwind of thoughts that can't seem to be stopped.

Choking is a decrease in performance due to too much perceived stress. You hear all the time how at the big games players choke. Mental stress rears its ugly head under the guise of physical tension. It can also be magnified if you feel that you play for approval of others, thus thinking that a bad performance would result in loss of approval. It all comes down to how you view a situation. How do you view clutch situations - as just another play? Don't see certain situation as pressure situations, view them as "just taking care of business." How you react in clutch situations will be a result of your perception and preparation. You need to interpret the situation as an opportunity to succeed, rather than a chance to fail. Peak performers love to be in these situations.

Then comes the physical consequences. You are so worried, unfocused and physically tense that there is no way you can let your natural instincts take over and be fluid in your movements. You tend to grip things tighter and have blurred vision. You fatigue prematurely because your breathing is short, rapid and shallow. As breathing gets shallower and shallower you then begin to literally "choke." The tension causes constricted muscles in the chest and throat, so you can't breath very well. There is no circulation of blood to your limbs. This is due to the fight or flight response, in that by cutting off circulation to your limbs, it will prevent you from bleeding to death. Unfortunately, in sports, this is a negative because it takes away from your ability to have a keen awareness of your body. You are tight and second guessing your every move, overthinking every single detail. You become so worried that you just freeze. Thus, you've choked.

The capability to stay focused on the task at hand, without worrying about all the external variables over which you have no control, is the primary goal in achieving peak performance and avoiding choking. Yet it seems athletes spend about 95% of their time worrying about those uncontrollables (i.e., field condition, opposing team, bad calls, etc.), rather than on the one thing over which you have absolute control 100% of the time - yourself, both mentally and physically.

What happens when you lose your focus, in practice or in a game (since this is the precursor to choking)? If you lose your focus in practice, you need to remember what it is you are trying to accomplish and move forward from that point. If you find that the negative thoughts are still creeping in, you can use:

1. **Imagery** – Take all your negative thoughts and fears and imagine crumpling them up into a ball and then throwing them away. Or, mentally put all those negative thoughts in your bag and zip it up. This way they are no longer a factor. Doing this puts **you** in control.
2. **Positive self affirmations** – If you find yourself saying something negative, reframe it into something positive ("I will get a hit"). Reframing allows you to change your point of reference. You are what you think. In sports this can be a problem or an opportunity – it's up to you. The higher your confidence is, the more that will lower your risk of choking. I can guarantee you, the more you fear choking, the more you'll choke.

If you lose your focus in a game (usually after you've made a mistake), you need to quickly let go of the error and move on. Have a **here and now approach**. Nothing is more important than what you are doing at that exact moment. Not the strike out at your first at-bat, or the interception you threw in the first quarter. Focus only on one thing at a time. Be aware of your optimal arousal level. Too little usually results in decreased alertness and motivation. Too much usually results in you psyching yourself out and makes you a prime candidate for choking.

To deal with the physical consequences of choking, you can do the following:

1. **Circle breathing** – Find an arbitrary place to focus on (i.e., 2nd base, spot on glove, field goal uprights) and take a deep breath slowly through your nose and exhale slowly through your mouth. Repeat this until you feel your body start to relax and your mind is clear. It should only take a couple of deep breaths (if this is something you practice regularly!). Make sure you use the same focal point each time – consistency is the key, it is the mark of a champion.
2. **Narrow your focus** – See only your target (i.e., catcher's glove, receiver's number on chest). This will help keep your focus on what you should be doing rather than what **might** happen.

As a coach, you need to be aware of putting extra pressure on players during games and key situations. Certain patterns of choking can be perpetuated by the coaches. ("You have to get a hit, we need you,"). This type of talk can reinforce the importance of a situation and the player will most likely not respond well.

Choking is something that can be constructively dealt with. It's up to you to not only be positive and control your thoughts, but also to have the self-awareness to know when things aren't going as they should and utilize all your tools and resources to turn the situation around. Reduce your tendency to choke – be prepared.

Slumps

Unfortunately, no one can be on a hot streak all season long – slumps are an inevitable part of sports. As soon as you realize this, you'll be in a better position to deal with it before it gets out of hand. What counts more than the mistakes themselves, is your reaction to them – you control whether that **one** mistake leads to another. The trick becomes how **you react** to one or two bad outings. Slumps last as long as you let them. You need to keep in mind that you have probably been in this situation before, and it most likely won't be the last time either.

What are slumps?

"Lament, if necessary, but do not dwell too long on your bad moments, lest they rise to rule your emotions forever" (Roberts, p. 88).

A slump is a decrease in performance that causes you to lose confidence in your abilities, thus keeping you performing at a level below your athletic potential. Basically, one bad performance snowballs into another, and is perpetuated by negative self-talk and tension. You seem to have no memory of all the times you did perform well. Your skills seem to just desert you. It is a prolonged period of time when you aren't performing well. The skills you thought you could count on are no where to be found and you are baffled by this.

What causes slumps?

1. Being more concerned about numbers – Quantity without quality is not a good thing! You are more worried about the results than the process. You become more "statistics" oriented rather than being concerned about the quality of your play. You feel as long as your numbers look good than everything is okay – that is the "important" thing.
2. Thinking too much or over analyzing when you should just be reacting and trusting your instincts. You become overanalytical and put too much pressure on yourself. You need to get out of your own way,

and trust your body and your mind. This will be easy to do if you've prepared mentally and physically.

3. Trying too hard – This results in stiff movement as opposed to natural, fluid motion. When you "try" you are thinking instead of reacting.

Simply put, slumps are caused by a player's response to **one** bad performance (i.e., poor field goal attempt, bad pitching appearance, error on a play, etc.). A loss in the ability to relax and focus, coupled with a loss of confidence and trust in your abilities, makes it very difficult for you to bounce back effectively. The first thing many players do is panic and adjust their mechanics, which can, more often than not, lead to further problems.

Then, each game gets more and more anxiety-provoking, which in turn makes you more nervous, which then starts to effect your self-confidence, and compounds the pressure you feel. Players usually feel their grip get tighter, and can feel overall tension because they are trying too hard. There is a difference between trying hard and giving 100%. Trying hard creates mental and physical tension, while giving 100% is pushing yourself to the outer limit of your capabilities. You don't want to force things that aren't there (i.e., throwing into bad coverage because you are desperate for a completion, swinging at a pitch way out of your strike zone because you are anxious to get a hit). You tend to get desperate and forget what works.

How to deal with slumps?

1. Don't make the mistake of asking 15 people for help, just ask one or two (most likely your direct coach). Otherwise you will be bogged down with too much information. You need to narrow your focus to what the situation requires and be positive and confident.

2. Rule out the physical - Assess if it is a flaw or a mistake. Flaws are a reoccurring error that needs readjustment, and a mistake is something that just happened and is not a usual occurrence. Do this by talking with your coach to see if you are making any mechanical errors. You don't want to introduce any technical changes if it isn't necessary. If there are no physical reasons, you can safely assume that it's in your mental approach. If you find that it isn't physical be sure not to overpractice, this can often introduce new problems that were never there to begin with.
3. Make a list with your coach – On one side is what you "are" doing when you are playing, and on the other side what you "should" be doing. Then, review the discrepancies. Go over everything - from what is **physically** going on before and during (are your muscles tight? are you moving fluidly?), to what is going on **mentally** (negative self-talk? distracted? unable to focus? no confidence?) As a coach, help your player become aware of what he is doing wrong. Where the breakdown occurs is the place you should focus most of your attention. Professor Emeritus, Dr. Bruce Ogilvie had this to say on the subject of slumps, "the athlete is not abiding by his gifts as he was before and you have to take time and define how the athlete has changed his behavior."
4. If you've narrowed down that it manifests itself in a physical way, practice using circle breathing (taking a couple of deep, slow breaths through your nose and out your mouth) before games and practices. Use circle breathing in potentially anxiety-provoking situations (i.e., the batter's box, while pitching, before a field goal or free throw). Do a quick check to make sure you are relaxed, and if not, go back and do a few more deep breaths.

5. If it manifests itself in a cognitive way, focus on your self-talk. Chances are you're saying things like "don't do this, don't do that," "I gotta," "I have to start concentrating harder." These statements just increase the pressure you're already putting on yourself. Positively reinforce yourself with things like "I know I can do this" and "I've done this many times before." Change the negative to positive. Also, visualize past experiences when you have executed your task perfectly. By reminding yourself of this, it will help in subsiding your doubts and getting your self-confidence back. Don't chastise yourself, that just creates more pressure and takes every last ounce of fun out of the game for you during this struggle.

When athletes say they are not comfortable at the plate, this often means they are not seeing the ball well. If an athlete is not seeing the ball well, it means that they are distracted by either their own thoughts or outside distractions, or that they are physically tight, which reduces the visual field. This is usually demonstrated by overswinging. They are, first of all, trying too hard, and secondly, not seeing the ball well which causes them to make decisions too late.

There's a difference between going up and striking out and going up and hitting the ball right to someone. But, we tend to lump them both together when we see the final result as 0-4 for the day. You can determine if you are in a slump or not by the quality of your at-bats. You need to know your capabilities, have a plan and believe in yourself. Make your assessment of the situation based on the facts, not ruled by emotion.

Many times slumps begin while you are hitting well. Let me explain, when you are hitting well you are less disciplined at the plate because you have the utmost confidence in your ability to hit **anything**. So what starts out as a good thing, can come back and bite you if you are not careful. That's why it is so important to not become complacent at the plate and stick to the good habits that have lent themselves to you hitting great in the first place.

Everyone will go through a slump at one time or another, only you can control the severity and length of it by your patience, concentration and mental attitude. As a coach, you need to reassure your athlete that they are still an asset to the team, even though they don't feel very productive at this time. For example, remind them how effective they are at playing defense, even though they are struggling at the plate. Also, in baseball and softball bunting can help a player out of a slump. This can help them get back in the groove and feel a part of the offense again. This increases confidence, concentration and gets players to stop chasing bad pitches.

During slumps you need to stay positive, in attitude and thought. Keep your focus on what you should and want to do, not on what you should be avoiding! By not panicking after one or two games, you can keep things in perspective; and although slumps may be a part of sports, you can take control and make sure they don't last long. You have the tools to help yourself, mentally and physically. Just go back to the basics. When there is a problem this is usually the best thing to do to get yourself back on track. Keep things simple and have fun! Stay within yourself and have a purpose for every move you make.

Injuries

Unfortunately, injuries are also a big part of sports. Every time you step out on the field or court you run the risk that you might sustain an injury. Not being able to play is probably every athlete's greatest fear. Although, if you do get hurt you can still practice – in your mind. In this section we will first address some of the things that you go through when you experience an injury and then move on to how you can be most productive during this time, so that you are well prepared when you are able to go back out there and play.

Sustaining an injury has an impact on all aspects of your life, not just in sports. It changes who you feel you are – for the time being anyway. For many though, an injury may be the first step in termination from your sport. Your level of self-esteem and intrinsic motivation effect your response to the injury, the rehabilitation process, and the possibility of termination.

When you get injured you tend to question your self-worth and your ability to get back to where you were, tending to focus only on the negative. You also may start to question your identity and role on the team. You lose your sense of invincibility. It is a blow to the ego and hard to see someone else doing your job. Mentally dealing with an injury can sometimes be more frustrating than the physical side of it.

What usually happens first is you deny that the injury is serious. You claim you are okay and still want to go out and play. When you realize that your body has another thing in mind, you get angry. You're mad at yourself, mad at the injury, mad at anybody around you. And you wonder, why did this have to happen to me? Why now? From there you tend to get down and depressed, realizing that even **you** are vulnerable to injury and that you are not invincible. Once you have gone through all of this you can then move forward to the rehabilitation process. You can put things in perspective and set a game plan to get back to where you need to be. You must realistically review and reassess your values, identity and role.

How to deal with an injury

1. Let yourself feel sad, mad and/or upset – Whatever emotions accompany your injury, don't repress anything, let it all out. Even if you hold it in for now, it will have to come out sooner or later.
2. Deal with what has happened, don't dwell on "if only." It won't do any good and chances are, that way of thinking will slow down your recovery time anyway.
3. Set new goals – Set rehabilitation goals for yourself. Be patient and just focus on the new goals you have set, not on past goals. Set goals you can succeed at and will help build your confidence level.
4. Positive attitude – If there was ever a time that you would benefit from a positive mental attitude, it is now. It can help speed up your rehabilitation process. Positive self-talk aids in your recovery from injuries.
5. Practice visualizing – If you practice visualization your nervous system remains in tune to your skills and you'll move along much quicker when you get the green light to start physically practicing again.
6. Do relaxation sessions – Relaxation improves the blood flow by dilating your blood vessels. This increased circulation to the injured areas is good for speeding up recovery time.
7. Seek out support – Do everything you can to stay involved with your team. Don't alienate yourself. Attend as many practices and games as possible. Do what you can to stay involved. For example, help shag balls, do charts, be a cheerleader, etc.
8. Keep the lines of communication open – Clear communication between you and your athletic trainer, you and your coach, you and your teammates is very important to the rehabilitation process.

9. Be patient – Take it one day at a time, don't rush back. Doing things in excess and extremes may be what led to the fatigue and injury in the first place. You don't want to return too early and risk getting injured again.

Mental training techniques can be used in a preventative approach to contribute to an injury-free environment. By mentally practicing you decrease your chances of injury due to the fact that you've taken away some of the emotional hassles that many times lead to strain, stress and injury. With stress and anxiety comes muscle tension, which may cause you to strain a muscle. When you are stressed you also have a shorter attention span and limited visual field, which also contribute to the possibility of injury. Injuries will happen soon enough, don't help it out along by being tired, stressed, or not focused – use these skills!

Conclusion

Hopefully you now have a better understanding of what it takes to build and maintain a good working team. One thing is unmistakable – it's takes time and energy to get where you want to go. It requires a choice on your part to stay committed for the duration. This will require a lot of hard work – but what a feeling when you accomplish your goals! Remember, it is not an on-again off-again thing. Consistency is the key to your success – consistency in your preparation and approach (mental and physical).

This book has shown you over and over the importance of mental training and how it relates to reaching peak performance. The correlation is so strongly evident. If you read this book in its entirety you can see how important the progression is, and how you must address each area if you are going to have a strong team and be a solid contributor. If each individual athlete does their part 100%, your team will be unstoppable!

You took a step by reading this book. Now what you must do is implement the exercises and techniques that were introduced. It will most likely take a lot of practice on your part, and it may seem difficult at first. And, in the beginning, it may also seem like it's not making any difference, but stick with it. Be consistent and repetitious in your practice and make these sports psychology techniques an ingrained part of your training. You want them to be second nature, just like your physical skills. Add these mental training skills to your daily practice and watch them become some of your greatest strengths and resources. All the time and effort you put in will come back to you ten-fold.

If you keep up the good work you are going to see positive results. Keep in mind, overnight change is not what it's about. It's about gradual change in the right direction. You probably aren't going to see any grave improvement overnight, but have faith you are headed down the right path. Keep your mission, your goals, and a clear picture of the kind of athlete you want to be in the forefront of your mind - this will help with your motivation. **Stay positive, be patient and good luck on this new journey you are starting!**

BIBLIOGRAPHY

Albinson, J. G., & Bull, S. J. (1990). A mental game plan. London, Ontario: Spodym. Book review: *The Sports Psychologist*, **4**, 76-77.

Arnold, G., & Straub, W. (1973). Personality and group cohesiveness as determinants of success among interscholastic basketball teams. *Proceedings of the Fourth Canadian Psycho-Motor Learning and Sport Psychology Symposium*, 346-353.

Barkley, C., & Johnson, R.S. (1992). *Outrageous*. New York, NY: Simon & Schuster.

Bennett, J. G., & Pravitz, J. E. (1982). *The miracle of sports psychology*. New Jersey: Prentice-Hall, Inc.

Bell, K. F. (1983). *Championship thinking*. New Jersey: Prentice-Hall, Inc.

Bradley, B. (1976). *Life of the run*. New York, NY: Quadrangle The NY Times Book Co.

Brennan, S. J. (1990). *Competitive excellence: The psychology and strategy of successful team building*. Omaha, NE: Peak Performance Publishing.

Bird, A., Foster, C., & Maruyama, G. (1980). Convergent and incremental effects of cohesion on attributions for self and team. *Journal of Sports Psychology*, **2**, 181-193.

Brawley, L., Carron, A., & Widmeyer, W. (1987). Assessing the cohesion of teams: Validity of the Group Environment Questionnaire. *Journal of Sports Psychology*, **9**, 275-294.

Bunker, L. K., Rotella, R. J., & Reilly, A. S. (Eds.). (1985). *Sports psychology*. Ann Arbor, MI: McNaughton & Gunn.

Carnegie, D. (1964). *How to win friends and influence people*. New York: Simon & Schuster.

Carron, A., & Ball, J. (1977). Cause effect characteristics of cohesiveness and participation motivation in intercollegiate ice hockey. *International Review of Sport Sociology*, **12**, 49-60.

Carron, A., & Chelladurai, P. (1981). Cohesion as a factor of sport performance. *Journal of Sport and Exercise Psychology*, **10**, 199-213.

Carron, A., Widmeyer, W., & Brawley, L. (1985). The development of an instrument to assess cohesion in team sports. *Journal of Sports Psychology*, **7**, 244-266.

Cartwright, D., & Zander, A. (1968). *Group dynamics: Research and theory*. New York, NY: Harper & Row.

Chieger, B. & Sullivan, P. (1990). *Football's greatest quotes*. New York, NY: Simon & Schuster.

Chopra, D. (1993). *The seven spiritual laws of success*. San Rafael, CA: Amber-Allen Publishing/New World Library.

Conner, D. (1988). *The art of winning*. New York: St. Martin's Press.

Corey, M., & Corey, G. (1987). *Groups: Process and practice*. Belmont, CA: Brooks/Cole Publishing Co.

Covey, S. R. (1990). *The 7 habits of highly effective people*. New York: Simon & Schuster.

Cratty, B. J. (1983). *Psychology in contemporary sports*. New Jersey Prentice-Hall.

Crumpacker, J. (1994, September 4). Rice's peerless work ethic turned him into TD Jerry. *San Francisco Examiner*, pp. C-1, C6-7.

Curtis, J. D. (1989). *The mindset for winning*. Wisconsin: Coulee Press.

Deci, E. L., & Ryan, R. M. (1985). *Intrinsic motivation and self-determination in human behavior*. New York: Plenum Publishing Corp.

Dorfman, H.A., & Kuehl, K. (1989). *The mental game of baseball: A guide to peak performance*. South Bend, IN: Diamond Communications, Inc.

Dowling, T. (1970). *Coach: A season with Lombardi*. New York: W.W. Norton & Company, Inc.

Fernandez, E. (1994, March 13). Sports shrinks help unravel hidden frailties. *San Francisco Examiner*, pp. A10-11.

Festinger, L., Schachter, S., & Back, K. (1950). *Social pressures in informal group*. New York, NY: Harper.

Fielder, F., Hartman, W., & Rudin, S. (1952). The relationship of interpersonal perception to effectiveness in basketball teams. (Suppl. Tech. Rep. No. 3, Contract N60T1-07135.) Urbana, IL: Bureau of Records and Services, Univ of IL.

Fielder, F. (1967). *A theory of leadership effectiveness*. New York: McGraw Hill.

Fisher, K., Rayner, S., & Belgard, W. (1995). *Tips for teams*. New York: McGraw Hill, Inc.

Freischlag, J. (1985). Team dynamics: implications for coaching. *Journal of Physical Education, Recreation and Dance*, **56**, 67-71.

Garfield, C. A. (1984). *Peak performance*. Los Angeles: Jeremy P. Tarcher, Inc.

Getts, M. (1996, August 10). Bring it on. *49ers Game Day Book*, pp. 17-18.

Gill, D. L. (1986). *Psychological dynamics of sport*. Champaign, Illinois: Kinetics Publishers, Inc.

Goldstein, B. (1981). The relationship between threat and cohesiveness on the process and outcome of basketball teams. Doctoral thesis, Univ of California, Los Angeles.

Greider, P. (1991, May 18). Gaining the mental edge. *Foster's Daily Democrat*, p. 17: Dover, NH.

Hall, D. M. (1960). *Dynamics of group action*. Danville, IL: Printers and Publishers, Inc.

Hacker, C., & Williams, J. (1981). Cohesion, satisfaction, and performance in intercollegiate field hockey. *Psychology of Motor Behavior and Sport. Monterey*, CA: NASPSPA.

Huang, C. A., & Lynch, J. (1992). *Thinking body, dancing mind*. New York, NY: Bantam Books.

Hill, N. (1972). *Think and grow rich action pac*. New York: Penguin Books USA, Inc.

Jackman, M. (1991). *Star teams, key player*. New York: Henry Holt & Company.

James, L., & Hartman, E. (1977). An examination of the relationships between psychological climate and VIE model for work motivation. *Personal Psychology*, **30**, 229-54.

Jones, M. (1974). Regressing group on individual effectiveness. *Organizational Behavior and Human Performance*, **11**, 426-451.

Joyner, F. G. (1996, July 19-21). Wisdom. *USA Weekend*, p. 6.

Katzenbach, J. R., & Smith, D. K. (1993). *The wisdom of teams*. Boston, MA: Harvard Business School Press.

Klein, M., & Christiansen, G. (1969). Group composition, group structure, and group effectiveness of basketball teams. *Sport, culture, and society: A reader on the sociology of sport*, 397-408.

Landers, D., & Lueschen, G. (1974). Team performance outcome and cohesiveness of competitive coacting groups. *International Review of Sport Sociology*, **9**, 57-69.

Lenk, H. (1969). Top performance despite internal conflicts. *Sport, culture, and society: A reader on the sociology of sport*, 393-397.

Levitt, E. (1965, June 13). Win for the UC track coach. *Tribune*, p. 51

Libo, L. (953). *Research center for group dynamics*. University of Michigan: Ann Arbor, Michigan.

Loy, J. (1981). *Sport and social systems.* Reading, MA: Addison-Wesley Publishing Co.

Lundy, J. L. (1992). *Teams - Together each achieves more success*. Chicago, IL: The Dartnell Corporation.

Martens, R. (1987). *Coaches guide to sports psychology.* Champaign, IL: Human Kinetics Publishers, Inc.

Martin, D. (1993). *TeamThink.* New York: Penguin Books.

McGrath, J. E. (1962). The influence of positive interpersonal relations on adjustment and effectiveness in rifle teams. *Journal of Abnormal and Social Psychology*, **65**, 365-375.

McNichol, T. (1996, July 19-21). What makes an Olympian? *USA Weekend*, pp. 4-14.

Mitchell, S. (1988). *Tao te ching* (Trans.) New York: HarperCollins Publishers.

Melnick, M., & Chemers, M. (1974). Effects of group social structure on the success of basketball teams. *Research Quarterly*, **45**, 1-8.

Murray, B. (1996, July). Psychology sails into the Olympic World. *The APA Monitor*, p. 6.

Murrell, A., & Gaertner, S. (1992). Cohesion and sports teams effectiveness: the benefits of a common group identity. *Journal of Sports and Social Issues*, **16**, 1-14.

Nideffer, R. M. (1976). *The inner athlete*. NY: Thomas Crowell.

Orlick, T. (1990). *In pursuit of excellence*. Champaign, IL: Human Kinetics Publishers, Inc.

Parker, G. M. (1990). *Team players and teamwork.* San Francisco, CA: Jossey-Bass Publishers.

Peterson, J., & Martens, R. (1972). Success and residential affiliation as determinants of team cohesion. *Research Quarterly*, **43**, 62-75.

Porter, K., & Foster, J. (1986). *The mental athlete*. New York: Wm. C. Brown Publishers.

Rainey, D., & Schweickert G. (1988). An exploratory study of team cohesion before and after a spring trip. *The Sports Psychologist*, **2**, 314-317.

Ravizza, K., & Hanson, T. (1995). *Heads up baseball*. Indianapolis, IN: Masters Press.

Ries, A. (1996). *Focus, the future of our company depends on it*. New York: Harper Collins Publishers, Inc.

Riley, P. (1993). *The winner within*. New York: G.P. Putman's Sons.

Robbins, A. (1986). *Unlimited power*. New York: Simon & Schuster.

Robbins, A. (1991). *Awaken the giant within*. New York: Summit Books.

Robbins, H., & Finley, M. (1995). *Why teams don't work*. Princeton, NJ: Petersons/Pacesetter Books.

Roberts, W. (1987). *Leadership secrets of Attila the Hun*. New York: Warner Books, Inc.

Ruder, M., & Gill, D. (1981). Immediate effects of win-loss on perception of cohesiveness in intermural and intercollegiate volleyball teams. Paper presented at NASPSPA Conference, Monterey, CA.

Russell, G. W. (1993). *The social psychology of sport*. New York, NY: Springer-Verlag, Inc.

Sartwell, M. (Ed.). (1994). *Napoleon Hill's keys to success*. New York: Penguin Books.

Scott, M. D., & Pelliccioni, L. (1982). *Don't choke: How athletes become winners*. Englewood Cliffs, NJ: Prentice-Hall, Inc.

Silva, J. (1984). *Psychological foundations of sport*. Champaign, IL: Human Kinetic Publishers, Inc.

Singer, R. N. (1986). *Peak performance and more*. New York: Mouvement Publications, Inc.

Sleek, N. (1996). Golf psychology: Mastering the mind game. *The APA Monitor*, p. 29.

Spink, K. (1990). Group cohesion and collective efficacy of volleyball teams. *Journal of Sport and Exercise Psychology*, **12**, 301-311.

Syer, J., & Connolly, J. (1984). *Sporting body, sporting mind*. New York, NY: Cambridge University Press.

Taylor, D., Doria, J., & Tyler, J. (1983). Group performance and cohesiveness: An attributional analysis. *The Journal of Social Psychology*, **119**, 187-198.

Tuckman, B. C. (1965). Developmental sequence in small groups. *Psychological Bulletin*, **63**, 384-399.

Tutko, T. & Tosi, U. (1976). *Sports psyching*. Los Angeles: Jeremy. P. Tarcher, Inc., a division of The Putnam Publishing Group.

Tzu. L. (1985). *The tao of leadership* (J. Heider Trans.). Atlanta, GA: Humanics Limited.

Tzu, S. (1963). *Sun Tzu the art of war* (S. B. Griffith, Trans.). New York: Oxford University Press.

Ungerleider, S., & Golding, J. M. (1992). *Beyond strength*. Dubuque, IA: Wm. C. Brown Publishers.

Vernacchia, R., McGuire, R. T., & Cook, D. L. (1992). *Coaching mental excellence*. Dubuque, IA: William C. Brown Communications, Inc.

Walton, G. M. (1992). *Beyond winning*. Champaign, IL: Leisure Press.

Walsh, B. (1990). *Building a champion*. New York: St Martin's Press.

Warren, W. E. (1983). *Coaching and motivation*. New Jersey: Prentice-Hall, Inc.

Weinberg, R. (1988). *The mental advantage*. Champaign, IL: Leisure Press.

Westre, K., & Weiss, M. (1991). The relationship between perceived coaching behavior and group cohesion in high school football teams. *The Sports Psychologist*, **3**, 41-53.

Widmeyer, W., Brawley, L., & Carron, A. (1985). *The measurement of cohesion in sports teams: The group environment questionnaire*. London, Ontario, Canada: Sports Dynamics.

Widmeyer, W., & Martens, R. (1978). When cohesion predicts outcome in sports. *Research Quarterly*, **49**, 372-377.

Williams, J. M. (Ed.). (1993). *Applied sports psychology*. Mountain View, CA: Mayfield Publishing Company.

Williams, J. M., & Hacker, C. M. (1982). Causal relations among cohesion, satisfaction, and performance in women's intercollegiate field hockey teams. *Journal of Sport Psychology,* **4**, 324-327.

Williams J., & Widmeyer, W. (1991). The cohesion-performance relationship in a coacting sport. *Journal of Sport and Exercise Psychology*, **13**, 364-371.

Yalom, I. (1983). *Inpatient Group Psychotherapy*. New York: Basic Books.

Yukelson, D., Weinberg, R., & Jackson, A. (1984). A Multidimensional Group Cohesion Instrument for Intercollegiate Basketball Teams. *Journal of Sports Psychology*, **6**, 103-117.

Zander, A. (1971). *Motives and goals in groups*. New York: Academic Press.

Zilbergeld, B., & Lazarus, A. (1981). *Mind power*. Boston: Little, Brown & Company.

INDEX

Are You WINNING THE MENTAL WAY?

Karle[...] schools, assoc[...]mation on th[...] rlene's avail[...]

Pleas[...] *g the Ment*[...]arlene Sugar[...]

Please[...] $1.00 for ea[...] $1.08 for sal[...]

Name ______________________________

Address ______________________________

City, State, Zip ______________________________

Quantity discounts are available to volume buyers, write for more info, or call Step Up Publishing at (650) 347-0826.